With much Aloha
& many blessings ♡

Gabrielle Olivier

AGE IS
NOT
A NUMBER

~~~~~~~~)(~~~~~~~

Getting OLD is All in Your Head

Gabrielle Olivier

*"All that we are is the result
of what we have thought."*
— Buddha

The Truth was in

Age

And Age was in

YOUth

— Trans-Siberian Orchestra

ACKNOWLEDGEMENTS

How can I possibly thank all those who have played a part on the stage of my sweet play of life. Some played leading men and women, others were called for support, and of course, there are countless walk-ons. Regardless of the role, you are all major players, gurus and teachers. But there is only one invisible force who plays the ultimate lead, who feeds my soul with whatever truth I am able to grasp at the time, and so . . .

I thank my Creator for allowing me to see, to feel, to visualize, to dream, to BE, and walk this earthly domain in love, peace, joy, blessings, anger, resentment, struggle, strife and gratitude for "it all." Thank you. Thank you. Thank you

Next, I wish to thank my beloved parents, Amy and Vincent, who brought me into this dimension we call Earth. They nourished, sacrificed and loved me dearly as their only child through every stage of my growth till they could stay no longer.

A special thank you to all leading men from my first love to the love of my life, Rob, who has shared my life experiences for 30 years. Deepest gratitude for my beloved son, Aaron, who has always been there for me through all my adult ups and downs, and for my baby Grant. who almost made it to two years of age. His tragedy exemplified the greatest teaching of my life. His story is told in my eBook, *Destiny's Moment of Forever.*

Thank you all who have challenged my professionalism in the world of career and continue to support my talents. A special thank you to all those who inspire me with their words of wisdom and examples thereof — all who became my friend as well as the many acquaintances whose name I never even learned. I am especially grateful for those who give me the opportunity to shine, in spite of how they choose to see me.

Thank you Jake Slater at BookBaby. You were a most patient helper guiding me through the entire process of preparing this manuscript for print. And thank you to Joe Maurer, a computer expert, who also patiently helped me through all my technical challenges.

Finally, I thank all my loving readers who continued to encourage me throughout this writing episode. And to all of nature for surrounding me with your wondrous scent, your willingness to feed and nourish me, your inspiration and glorious spread of color, form and great example of continuing to grow and move forward regardless of human greed, ignorance and disrespect.

CONTENTS

Aloha … (Hawaiian for hello/goodbye,
I love you, and so much more)   1

BEfore BEginning   2

On Stage   3

THE PROLOGUE   4

HAPPY   5

The 7th Sense   12

THE DRIVER'S LICENSE   14

Elder-child   18

ACT 1 — POEM: The Awakening   20

The Symphony   23

A Mother's Point of View   26

The Worldlings   27

Act 11 — POEM: The Discovery   28

Getting It Together   29

THE ART OF LIVING   30

About Creation   30

LOVE & FEAR   34

Choosing Your Way   35

Fear of Dis-ease   38

LOVE & MARRIAGE   40

STRESS   41

THE ART OF LETTING GO   43

Addiction to Vanity   45

Pseudo Beliefs   47

CREATING BLOBS IN YOUR LIFE 48

    Beauty of a Blob 49

    Reminiscing 55

    Thank You 58

    Destiny of a Cloud 61

HEALTH

    A Mother's Tragic Claim 63

    The Night Sweeps Me Away 76

APPEARANCE

    My Mask is Missing 78

ACT 111 — THE SENIOR MOMENT 84

    Eternity 87

    Truth Is 88

    As Time Marches On 90

EXPECTATIONS 94

    Expect What, When? 95

    The Mystery of Duality 96

ACT 1V — THE ELDER 100

    The Finish Line 105

EPILOGUE 107

    The Cleansing 110

MORE 111

ADDITIONAL INSPIRATION 112

    Maintaining Youth 114

Aloha

Please be aware this book is
not a map to the fountain of youth.
It's not a 'How to Stay Young' book.
It is not a 'how to' book of any kind.
It is simply a record of a few clues
I've found along the way.

So who am I?

Well, I'm not a scientist, a PhD or even a college graduate.
I'm a wife, mother, grandmother, self taught, professional
artist, interior designer, poet and writer living in Kauai,
Hawaii. So in brief, I'm just another soul playing my
part along this journey we call life. I'm a bit older
than most, and though I've paid attention to a lot
of clues in my quest of
"Searching for Truths that don't Lie"
I've found it's not enough to know.

So now, I'd love to share my
discoveries in and of 3D
and Living Color and
together, strive to
awaken to our
ONE
true self . . .

BEfore BEginning

Without even realizing
We spend our whole life wandering
To remember our way
Back
BEfore womb
BEfore birth
BEfore
BEginning

Obsessed with
Seeking, forever seeking
To find our twin flame to feel
Whole
To procreate
Expand
Express
Our "agony and ecstasy"
In a temporal world
Of pseudo reality

We pretend to
Be separate
To be someone else
Somewhere else
In a parade of disguise
Climbing
Praying
Falling
Rising
Trying

Always trying
To remember our way
Back home
BEfore womb
BEfore BEginning

*Life in this dimension comes in stages
from innocent infant to the wise elder until our
light flickers and dims to shine no more.*

*Names for these familiar growth periods
vary, and each stage offers a new
and different scenario.*

*A learned actor releases he/r props
and costumes at the closing of every scene
willingly moving on to the next with grace, style
and gratitude for the part. And that's
important to remember.*

*It's just a part on this great stage
we call Earth under the spot light
of the sun day in and day out.*

THE PROLOGUE

William Shakespeare said it most artfully:
"All the world is a stage. Play your part well."

YOU ARE THE STAR

on this stage of a Four Act Play. The ongoing story

seems as though it will last forever. You were always on

borrowed time as the star, producer, director and even writer

of your own play, but maybe this is the scene where you finally

Get it.

Hopefully, you have lived through enough comedy and drama

that you are able to reach a point of integration, integrating

the physical with the mental and spiritual selves

finding perfect balance on the tight rope

we call

L

I

F

E

HAPPY

"What is the the common wish of humankind?"
My spiritual teacher asked.

"Happiness," a student answered.
"Yes, Happiness," she smiled.

We've all heard of those famous, one named people like Cher, Madonna, Sting and others, but how many have heard of *Happy*? I first met Happy while working as a designer at a leading furniture store on the island of Kauai, Hawaii. I remember a tall slender woman, impeccably dressed in unique, fashionable clothing cheerfully walking towards me. "Hi, you must be Gabrielle, I'm *Happy*," she said, flashing a wide, brilliant smile.

"I brought you a newspaper." She handed me a folded paper. "I'm the ad representative for the Garden Isle News. I heard you're in charge of advertising," she said, beaming, "so, we'll be working together."

After a brief meeting, I recognized that Happy loved her work, loved creating her ads — she even loved the pressure and the deadlines. She found all the usual dreaded challenges of advertising fun and exciting. Almost immediately, Happy and I became best lunch buddies. For more than ten years, long after I had left the furniture store, Happy and I shared a zillion experiences and feelings over periodic lunch breaks from *it all*.

"Who gave you the name Happy?" I once asked.

"It started as a nickname when I was a little girl. People just started calling me Happy because I was so, well . . . *happy.* I just don't let things bother me. Life is too short, I'd rather be happy."

A widow and mother of three, Happy lived alone in a private apartment in her eldest daughter's home. She was a voracious reader, very active and loved to play golf and tennis. She was shocked by anyone who would insinuate she was too old to play, too old to work, or too old for any energetic endeavor. Happy would never tell her age, not even to me. She told me she wasn't her numbers.

"I never tell anyone," she said, and why should she? Happy was bursting with energy. Age didn't appear to exist for Happy.

She reminded me of someone from another time. No one dressed like Happy, especially in Hawaii. She wore long sleeves and long skirts almost down to her ankles with coordinated white or dark nylons, 2" heels with pointed toes and matching bag. Her short, perfectly cropped hair was colored champagne blond, a striking contrast with her tanned skin, thick black eyebrows and sparkly brown eyes. More importantly, you could always depend on Happy's peppy persona and brilliant smile. They called her *Duchess* at Starbucks. I often called her, *Her Happiness.*

I believe one of her secrets to happiness was her sincere interest in others. Never one to be self centered and talk about herself, she always wanted to know about me, as if I led some kind of exciting, superstar life.

Happy always saw the beauty in everything and everyone – never had an unkind word to say about anyone, even when someone was mean to her. She was eternally grateful for it all, the good and the bad. Nothing appeared to disturb *Her Happiness,* and if it did, she never bothered to discuss it. If *Her Happiness* sounds like a perfect person, I guess in many ways, she was, at least to me.

"Baby Doll, I'm going to be in your neighborhood today, can we meet for lunch?" Happy often called me Baby Doll.

When arriving at the restaurant, she was already waiting, sitting perfectly straight . . . as always. Almost immediately, she explained that she had been on a leave of absence due to some health issues.

"OMG! I had no idea. It can't be serious," I remarked. "You look radiant and beautiful as ever."

"Well," she paused gazing thoughtfully out the window, "I've got some things to go through. I'm going to Oahu for an MRI tomorrow. I'll have to go back and forth for some treatments for a while, but I'll be fine."

I politely probed to learn about her condition, but I knew she wouldn't discuss anything personally and potentially negative about herself so I didn't push it, just carried on as normal.

Although Happy was her usual cheerful self, there was a little voice inside trying to tell me this would be my last lunch with Happy, but I couldn't go there. This couldn't possibly be the last lunch with Happy. She was glowing. It had to be my fear talking.

"Promise me one thing," she called from behind on our way to the lady's room.

"Sure, what?"

"Don't tell anyone how old you are because you don't look anywhere near your age, not that you're old now, but age has a stigma, and the older you get people will look at you differently, and since you aren't your numbers, you never need to tell."

We stood before the mirror over two separate lavatories. In spite of her bright spirit, her deep lines and physical tell tale signs of age always led me to wonder just how old she was beneath that glow. Why wouldn't she just tell me? I wouldn't tell anyone.

"I'll have to think about that," I replied, wiping my hands dry, "but I do know what you mean." We hugged and said goodbye. She promised to call and keep me posted on her progress. I felt her eyes follow me as I walked away.

I had misplaced Happy's home number so after a couple of weeks I called the newspaper. They weren't allowed to pass her number on, but they would give her 'my' number. Twice, I called to leave a message; still, no word from Happy.

Shortly thereafter, the newspaper ran a feature article on me. I thought for sure the article would prompt her to call with predictable praise and congratulations. Silence prevailed. When I stopped by the office to pick up some copies of the article, I asked . . .

"Does anyone know how Happy is doing?"

"Yes, she's doing great," one of the girls at the front desk replied. "She'll be back to work on Monday. I heard she's real excited about coming back. She even bought new clothes."

I was thrilled that Happy would be back in two days; still, I had this nagging feeling she wouldn't make it, but two days was only a weekend away. I immediately pushed the thought aside and left another message for her to call me. Tuesday morning — a call from the newspaper . . .

"Gabrielle, you left a message for Happy to call you. I'm so sorry Gabrielle, but Happy passed away over the weekend." The words struck like a cold knife to slice a little piece of my heart. How was that possible? I couldn't believe it, even though deep inside, I knew . . . I knew. Did she . . . know?

I felt cheated. I didn't have a chance to discuss this with her. Why didn't she call me? What had she gone through? Why did she die? How could she just leave without saying goodbye to me? She was so alive, so beautiful, so ... *happy*. It didn't seem possible that I would never see Happy's smile or hear her kind words of encouragement ever again.

It also didn't seem possible that Happy left me here to drive the streets and carry on with the trite obligations of the material world without our lunch breaks from *it all*.

"Do you know how she died?"

"No, no one seems to know, but it was sudden and peaceful. There's an article in today's paper."

I was on my way to give a decor consultation at a leading resort with no time to cry. Happy wouldn't want me to cry. Suddenly, I felt like I had to mirror *Her Happiness*. She had left me a great gift, an amazing legacy, and she had willed it to everyone she knew.

By her very existence, she had shown us all how to love and to BE happy. Like my father, I've always been pleasantly happy, but there are levels and degrees of happiness, and true happiness is a natural state of remaining happy no matter what is going on around you.

"HAPPY LIVED UP TO HER NAME" the headline read on the front page of the paper. There was no age or cause of death revealed, only a picture of her familiar beaming face and many words of praise from her co-workers.

Two days later a bigger headline appeared to simply read H A P P Y above a full page tribute. I stared at the big HAPPY font spread across the top of the page, then read all the words of praise and gratitude for *Her Happiness*. I wondered why no one made a big deal about *Her Happiness* before. I wondered why they didn't put her name on the front page with a story of her good deeds, or a full page of so many testimonies when she was alive. Why did we all just take her constant glow of happiness for granted?

Happy didn't leave a list of great accomplishments, a worldly fortune and shelves of awards. Happy wasn't an artist, musician or major talent of any kind. She didn't politic or strive to save the world. Happy didn't study with any masters or engage in spiritual practices. She wasn't a searcher and seeker of truth. She *was* the truth. The headline with her well deserved name revealed her purpose: the common wish of humankind, to be . . . HAPPY.

There is a famous Zen saying: "Before enlightenment, chop wood and fetch water. After enlightenment, chop wood and fetch water." Like a true master, Happy simply went about chopping wood and fetching water from moment to moment in love and light. Is there really any greater art form? How blessed I am to have known her. How special to have been her friend.

Though Happy and I will never meet for lunch again, I was not left without food for thought. Happy had truly exemplified how to bridge Heaven and Earth, humbly demonstrating the difference between the struggle of BEcoming something or someone, and the reward of simply BEing the true self, living the art of happiness in the now of forever.

There was no date of birth on Happy's gravestone.
I would never know how old she was.

The 7ᵗʰ Sense

Ego's born like
A hole in the soul
Deepened in guise to
Identify the 7th sense of
"Wonder"
Glistening in young eyes.

Desire follows birth on earth
Desire to love, to taste, to touch, to speak
To walk, to run, to conquer, to know.
Dare to spend your whole life
Seeking to fill the hole.

Should disappointment swell
From lack of any source
And desire fails
To yield as before —
Lest not give up or in
For verily when . . .
The 7th sense of
"Wonder"
Dies
In your eyes

You are reduced to
~ Old ~
Before your time.

An Everlasting Sense of Wonder . . .

The late actress, Elizabeth Taylor, was once considered the most beautiful woman in the world. I recall observing her wide eyed sense of wonder, and determined it was her expression that gave her such a youthful ambience throughout her memorable movie career. I was disappointed there was such little hoopla when she died. I mean, we had just lost one of the most beautiful women in the world, but the world had moved on to younger beauties of the time . . . still, I will be forever inspired by the memory of the sense of wonder in her eyes.

The Promise I Couldn't Make . . .

Happy's life of "not telling" her age gave me a lot to think about. How long can one really hide behind a number? When does a woman admit her age to all? Men always tell. And what do you do when your grandchildren are no longer children, but young men and women? How can you reveal the age of your children who have grown past 50 years without revealing your own numbers?

My age had remained a mystery to all my poet friends on the internet, believing as Happy had warned: "There's a stigma attached to age." It's true that in some cultures age means you've had enough time to accumulate a little wisdom, so age is a good thing, but America seems to have little respect for the "old" man or woman. Wisdom is not really a priority, a symbol of suck-cess. America is devoted to youth. Just ask the friendly Botox man.

"I am not my numbers!"
Happy
Happily exclaimed.

I flashed back to a lunch with Happy when she had said: "I'm even older than you," as if that was a really BIG number, and of course it was/is according to American standards. I also flashed back to a time in Verizon when the young assistant handed me my new iPhone and asked me to put in my date of birth. I remember thinking how long it seemed to get *alllllllll* the way back to 1937. And then . . .

THE DRIVER'S LICENSE

June 16, 2014

The day arrived to apply for a new driver's license. Finally, I had all the right paperwork. All I had to do was pass the eye exam. To be honest, all that paper work was kinda testy, especially when the nice lady behind the big imposing table said, "Well you didn't fill in the most important information."

"I didn't?"

"No, you forgot your name and address. See, right here." She pointed to lines two and three.

"Geez! I really thought I had it all together," I lamented

feeling all embarrassed. After altering the page, and providing the two lines with my name and current address, she got to the part of when I needed to reapply, which was in another two years. At that point, she looked astonished.

"HOW OLD ARE YOU?" She boldly asked, looking at me then back to the computer screen.

"76," I replied, with no sound of apology. I mean, I was talking to a lady with all my numbers in her face.

"Oh, my God! I'm totally shocked. I would never have guessed it. I thought you were at least 20 years younger." Quickly, I subtracted 20 from 76 in my head.

"56, that's a good number," I said, smiling, remembering when the thought of becoming 50 really sounded *old.*

"I had no idea till the computer said you have to reapply within another two years. I thought it had to be a mistake. You should WRITE A BOOK ON AGING, but be sure to put your picture on the cover because that will prove you know what you're talking about. You could call it *How to Age,* or *Secrets of Aging,* well. . . " she paused, "you're the writer, you'll think of something."

"I could call it *The Art of Aging,"* I suggested before remembering writing a poem of the same title, and when I posted it on my poet's site — hardly anyone read it. I was so surprised because there are so many elders on the site. Maybe they thought I was too young to know any secrets because I've only shared a recent picture and never revealed my age.

"I could call it . . . . *GOIN' ON 80* with a subtitle: *But What's in a Number?"*

"Oh, that's good. That would do. I can't believe you're 76. It must be positive thinking; you seem very positive."

"It's about keeping the energy high." I was surprised at my comment and how intently she listened. Somehow, I knew I wasn't supposed to be surprised, but I was.

"You'd have to explain that to me, but that's what the book will be all about, right?"

"Right. I'll be sure to bring you a copy, a signed copy."

"I'm 59," she admitted. "I can hardly wait till I'm 62 and can retire."

"You see . . . "I never use the word "retire." It sounds like I got tired, quit to rest, and will never, ever work again."

"Oh my, I never thought of it that way," she admitted.

"Well, I've been changing careers my whole life — like this morning I woke up an Interior Designer, and now, because of you, I'm off to write my book about aging. I'm not retiring from anything, just on to something else. Know what I mean?

"I do," she agreed.

"Meanwhile, thank you for the boost of inspiration."

We completed our transaction and bid our aloha. I never dreamed that applying for my driver's license would be such a positive, life changing experience which only goes to prove . . . it doesn't do any good to dread anything because you never know what treasure the experience will reveal.

Every situation provides opportunity for growth.

My new found friend was right. Why hide behind a pseudo age of 56? Who cares? I'm' even past the age of caring. What am I saving myself for?

Growing Up VS. Getting Old

How many times have you heard someone say, "I never want to grow up," and so, when given the opportunity to grow, they whine and complain about being a victim, which leaves all that's left is getting OLD, because no matter how you cut it, we do grow older, and that's a good thing, I mean, who wants to spend a lifetime crawling around in diapers? But we don't have to get OLD.

> " Aging is one thing, growing up another.
> What is the meaning of growing up? Taking all the
> responsibility, good and bad - whatsoever happens to
> you, you are responsible for it."
> — Osho

We are seldom aware of what we put into motion. If we are aware, we seldom want to assume the responsibility. We tend to hide behind the curtain of our own plot as if no one sees, hears or cares. We seem to enjoy the act of pretending — of attaching the consequences of our actions on to "them." The only problem is, consciously or subconsciously, we DO know the difference, and that deep knowing can eat away at our hearts and souls to make us old before our time.

Elder-child

Within every new born
an old soul longs for your
Love
to celebrate life and feel safe
firmly grasping any finger
of your hand.

Within every elder
A little child longs for your
Love
to celebrate life and feel safe
walking along your side
holding your hand.

Copyright © Gabrielle, 01/07/2014

*"We can easily forgive a child
who is afraid of the dark
the real tragedy is when men
are afraid of the light."*
— Plato

WHAT DO I MEAN
BY KEEPING THE ENERGY HIGH?

Since we live in a dimension of seeming duality, it's often easier to define what is not as opposed to what is. Keeping the Energy High is not a form of religion, technology, high living, or even faith. Keeping the Energy High is a conscious way of living, and it's never too soon or too late to start watching what you put into motion. Once, in a meditative conversation with my inner guru, S/he said:

"Self-realization is your only purpose for BEing."
How do I reach the Path of Self-realization? I asked.
"There is nothing to reach," the wise one replied.
"YOU, are the path."

The Japanese, Spiritual practice of Mahikari, teaches that we are not a body, but a spirit with a mind and body — which means spirit first, mind subordinate, body follows. I felt that to be an extremely profound teaching since advertisements always list Body, Mind and Spirit in that order of awareness.

The following stories and information will cover the three subjects of Spirit, Mind and Body, so let us begin with —

ACT 1

The Awakening

A soul
Moves through a
Soft, warm, dark tunnel
Into a cold, bright hard space
Disconnected, left on it's own
No longer one, freedom to roam
Wet and afraid, destined to face

A strong case
Of cosmic amnesia

As we rip
Through the veil into the
Dream
It seems as though
We've come from very far
Can't remember
Why
Can't remember
Who we are

Open in heart
Completely
Numb to mind
We feel a sense of wonder
We are new
We are born
We're alive
We feel

~TORN~

As if a spell has been cast

What does it mean ~
This three-dimensional
Field of dream
How long will it
LAST
Last
Last
^^^
^^^
^^
?

Thus begins the grand illusion
From the first moment
We open the windows of our
Sleep filled eyes

Something's missing
An unknown part
In the equation
Neither dark nor light
True or false
Wrong or right
There
Is

BLISS

And Bliss simply
~ IS ~
Till it comes to end
In the fun filled game of

~ Let's Pretend ~

A soul's form of play
In its spirit of adventure
Leading to illusion
And the ultimate conclusion
IT'S ALL REAL
Real
Real
Real
∧∧∧
∧∧
∧

⤸ ☯ ⤹

WHAT DO I MEAN
BY KEEPING THE ENERGY HIGH?

At this point in time, there is still much debate as to how life began: who, where, why, when? Many appear to agree that conscious energy is the underlying source of creation — also that energy emits a vibratory frequency. Some animated vibrations are prone to reach higher and further than others depending on the awareness of each entity. So, are you reaching UP aspiring to the fullness of all you can be? Are you vibrating love, abundance, happiness, health and longevity, or are you trapped in a low vibration of settling for less?

It's always your choice. However low, you are totally equipped to change your circumstance. The disabled and disadvantaged who perform awesome, undeniable feats prove that will is stronger than lack. It all depends on you, your personal view and determination. Will you rise to reach the top of the mountain or allow the mountain to defeat and even bury you?

The Symphony

"To lead a symphony, you must turn your back on the crowd."
—Unknown

If one note emerges out of sync, the
entire uni-verse sings out of tune.

When all notes
are united in harmony
the whole symphony
crosses
the bridge
of peace
to a standing
ovation.

Copyright © Gabrielle, 09/16/2014

The Art of Balance . . .

The greatest challenge in life and perhaps the most significant is to learn how to balance our spiritual, mental and physical needs. Most all religions are based on inspiring beliefs. It's not necessary to belong to any one order in particular to appreciate, and even live by some of the amazing teachings like: "Except ye be converted, and become as little children, ye shall not enter into the kingdom of heaven."

Although heaven is a debatable and relative concept, what exactly does it mean to become as little children? It's obvious the overall premise doesn't mean to ACT childish, which is a totally different intention and direction, often uncontrollable, inconsiderate and obnoxious. It's advised we transform to *BEcome* as little children. In spite of a seeming obsession with demanding attention, we are born with . . .

Humility

There is so much talk about humility, and it seems so few really know what humility means. Again, since we relate to a duel reality, false pride and vanity would serve as the opposite of humility. For a little child, there's a whole world out there to discover, to taste, to feel, to explore. In the beginning, we explore for the pure sake of discovery. There is no secret agenda; no plot or plan; no reason or intention to explore for awards and recognition — to be the first, the biggest and the best. All that is beyond comprehension to a little child. Up to age three, we have yet to learn about pseudo pride and vanity — caring not how we appear to the outside world, we are humble in active practice. Ego's image has yet to birth, which brings us to . . .

Trust

Trust is a lot like faith without the boundaries of a religion, practice or philosophy. For most adults, it's difficult to imagine that no harm can come to you when daily news blasts one disaster after another showing the world at large rioting and struggling to end and escape the atrocities of war. In the safety of our home, reclining on our cushy couch in front of our TV, we watch frantic heroes rush through chaotic crowds carrying stretchers with wounded and dying victims of violent attacks.

We watch nature's wrath: tornados, floods, fires, hurricanes, earth quakes, illness and plagues happen to other nice people. We can't help but secretly wonder and worry how such events can possibly happen to nice people like us, people who have faith and believe in God. A little child is seldom aware of such disasters, but a little child is aware of pain, suffering and size, aware that grown ups, places and things are often scary, overpowering and even threatening. Generally, a little child automatically trusts to feel the giant who lives within them is real, and will always be there to guide and protect them.

Forgiveness

It's easy to say you forgive someone on the surface, quite another to deeply feel it to the point of forgetting, a major key in the art of forgiveness. A little child is free of all that clutter, shame, guilt, memory and so called "reasoning of mind," and so, a little child need never forgive nor be forgiven. In the beginning we are too busy living to be affected by skin color, culture, division and enemies.

Around seven years of age, the age of reasoning arrives like a genie on a magic carpet. Suddenly, we can tell the difference between our imagination and what's really *out there*. Our light of innate wisdom fades, though we are convinced it has expanded to grow brighter than ever before. New dreams and thoughts emerge. One might think: *If it needs fixing, I'll be the one to fix it, to change it, heal it. I'll be the ONE.*

Osho, the once famous Indian Guru, claims we don't remember the first three years of our life because we are totally ourself, still living in the joyful *present* before we have been stamped with rules and acceptable behavior of society. This thought reminds me of an experience that enabled me to witness society's first stamp on my three year old son.

A Mother's Point of View . . .

When my son was three years old
a five year old neighbor boy
the son of an attorney man
would slam the door on my baby when he would knock to play

> He was older
>
> He was bigger
>
> He could read

When my son was five and a three year old knocked on our
door to play — my boy slammed the door on that baby
because that's what had happened to him

> It was his turn to be 'big'
>
> his turn to pay back
>
> and so it begins . . .

The beast rises within innocence to stamp its mark of darkness

> on a pure white soul
>
> igniting the innate fire of ignorance
>
> opening the door to cruel reactions

and so it goes . . .

In the words of Krishnamurti, another famous guru:

"It's possible to think that we're spiritually and mentally healthy because we share our mistaken values and understandings with those around us.

"Collectively, our ill minds create a society that is itself ill, and we consider ourselves healthy because our values are reflected in our fellow Worldings" . . .

"But mom, everyone is going.
Everyone is doing it!"

We all said it when growing up.
We've all heard it from our children
and they will hear it from their children
and so the wheel turns to create a world on
repeat
repeat
repeat

"But mom, everyone is going.
Everyone is doing it!"

For some reason this makes it all okay

to young minds of any age

no matter

what season of growth

"Everyone is going.

Everyone is doing it!"

ACT 11

The Discovery

Trekking through a typical life adventure
In a funny kind of pseudo light, we
Agree to embrace the night as
The game changes face ~
Place and appeal

~ Now ~
We're hooked on desire
Lookin' for love, for riches
And fame ~ a way to make a mark
Seeking goals and gain, a glorious way
To claim our name, and then we feel the pain
PAIN
Pain
Pain
∧∧∧
∧∧
∧

Funny, how we start with BEing and have to run
through all the BEcomes to get back to BEing —
if we ever do, in this lifetime anyway.

In the meantime, personally and collectively, we roam over the mindscape of imaginings. There is so much to GET TOGETHER . . . so much to . . .

Get Right
Get Tight
Get Loose
Get Ready
Get Lucky
Get Ahead
Get Rich
Get Big

GET
GET
GET

Get In
Get Up
Get Down
Get Hitched
Get Wheels
Get Around
Get Home
Get Stuff
Get Real
Get Lost
Get OUT
Get a Grip
Get Over
IT!

During the 60's everyone ran around talking about "IT" a lot. The big question was where "IT" was "AT" — some said it was behind the AT, others believed in the words of the Master Jesus, "Seek and ye shall find."

We are constantly challenged to understand
if and why we have to suffer in order to "Get It."

THE ART OF LIVING

"Perhaps creating keeps you young.
There is no 'time' when you are in a creating space.
The more of this world's time that you spend there,
the less you age."
— *David Mack, Rubuki: The Alchemy*

So, maybe all we need do is allow the inspiration of our Divine Creator to guide us through eternal life, listen to our inner voice, and follow our natural instincts all the way home.

About Creation . . .

When discovering the art of creativity
I admired many legendary artists like Michelangelo
Lautrec, Van Gogh, Isadora Duncan, Oscar Wilde and others.
They all suffered deeply.

Van Gogh even cut off his ear
obviously, because he didn't wish to hear, 'something.'
I wondered and wondered if I had to suffer to be a great artist.

I call myself an artist, but we are all artists
even setting a dinner table is a form of art.

I call myself a writer and a poet
but we are all writers scripting our poem of life
from moment to moment.

I call myself a dancer, but we are all dancers
every move we make is a form of dance, sometimes graceful
sometimes not.

I seldom paint, write or dance in attempt to create a conscious
work of art because I'm lonely or dissatisfied.
I tend to create because something in or around me is so
wondrous I am inspired to do so.

And even though many masters of art
may have suffered, it was still the depth of their love
that cried for expression.
It was love that forced its will
through the maze of fear and self destruction
to construct a masterpiece.

All ideas, great or small
pour forth from the love of the Creator
the source of our being

cradled deep within the well of soul, the

One True Master who graciously inspires

and encourages us to discover

experiment and surrender to our inherent destiny

as co-creators of life —

the greatest art form of all.

I encourage everyone to be conscious of their daily artistry

to watch and feel how the energy flows from mind to heart

moment to moment in the simplest of tasks, because truly

to conceive, create and move from a space of awareness

is to be in love, dancing . . .

with the Creator.

It's safe to say that any form of personal expression is
a significant key to self discovery, and if taken to a
positive level of experience, a BIG key
to youth and vitality.

I was fortunate that various forms of traditional artistic possibilities came with my package, not only as a means of self discovery, but lifelong self support and recognition. But life is full of surprises, and sometimes opportunity arrives in a completely unexpected package. As an only child I wanted to be "out there" admired, adored, a rich and famous ballerina, an actress or a princess. I never once dreamed of being an artist behind the scenes.

As fate would have it, I've yet to enact a lead in a play anywhere, even in high school. My mother said ballerinas get muscles and lead lonely lives, and my father said it was silly, so ballet lessons never happened. I did meet a prince once when assisting my husband to arrange an extravagant Hawaiian Honeymoon for a young Arabian Prince and his beautiful bride.

At eighteen, I stumbled onto a job as a commercial artist in my home town of Wichita, Kansas. Art just happened to me. Again, I never, ever dreamed of becoming an artist. I felt the job would suffice until I moved to L.A. where I was sure to be discovered, for *what,* I didn't know. It was rumored the sex goddess, Lana Turner, was discovered sipping a soda in the once famous Schwab's Drugstore. Even though her discovery was long before my time, and I was no Lana Turner, I can't tell you how much time I spent sipping sodas in Schwab's Drugstore. When the owner *retired* and closed the store in 1983, Lana Turner reported the legend was not true. She was discovered sipping a soda in the Top Hat Cafe. Never been there.

Commercial art taught me the value of letting go
of my attachment to personal creations labeled fine.
Later, my architectural/interior design and decor
business taught me not to confuse the form,
or business with my soul's purpose.

No matter how old, a true artist never retires
they will only change direction seeking a new
horizon along the path of self expression.

Don't forget we are all artists
from setting the dinner table
to painting the Mona Lisa.

LOVE & FEAR

"There are two basic motivating forces: love and fear. When we are afraid, we pull back from life. When we are in love, we open to all that life has to offer with passion, excitement, and acceptance like a child when life is new. We need to learn to love ourselves first, in all our glory and our imperfections. If we cannot love ourselves, we cannot fully open to our ability to love others or our potential to create. Evolution and all hopes for a better world rest in the fearlessness and open-hearted vision of people who embrace life."

— *John Lennon*

Fear
Asks why
Love knows

Fear
Demands and expects
Love accepts

Fear
Is jealous and controls
Love transcends

Fear
Raves and complains
Love listens

Fear
Judges and condemns
Love endures

Fear
Seeks revenge
Love forgives

Fear
Hangs on
Love flies

F
R
E
E

LOVE & FEAR: Copyright © Gabrielle, 2009

It's important to recognize the subtle deception of fear as opposed to love and trust. It's equally important to recognize that love and fear cannot stroll side by side, hand in hand. Maybe that's what the Bible means when it states: "You cannot serve two masters at the same time."

Choosing Your Way

When you come to the edge of a cliff
and get too close, you have a choice . . .
You can turn to Fear and be afraid of falling
or you can turn to Caution and simply
Watch where you are going

~~~~~~~~~~~~~<>~~~~~~~~~~~~

Fear is old, weak, crooked, decrepit and
Temporal
Caution is vigilant, concerned, watchful and
Immediate
Love is strong, straight, driven and
Eternal

Copyright © Gabrielle, 12/26/2013

Thinking Makes It So . . .

Remember, YOU are the path.
If fear leads your journey, it is your creative choice
to follow your fear.

Unfortunately, we believe we have been marked from the beginning of time. Many believe it's all about Adam and Eve who disobeyed God to eat of the Tree of Knowledge.

Whatever the origin, *fear* is there. On guard, we are afraid of not getting what we want and need, or afraid of losing what we already have – instinctively, we are ready to attack or defend. In this way we are more animal than human.

My mother brought me up on the teaching of James Allen and his booklet, *As a Man Thinketh.* Later I realized that before we choose how we act, what we eat, drink or do, the idea is first conceived in our mind. A conscious person will choose wisely. A conscious person who comes from a space of love and light won't have to worry about eating bad foods, or doing bad things. Love doesn't hate, lie, kill, steal, covet or harm anyone or anything in any way. Thought forms the idea, the idea arouses desire, desire creates action, and action materializes the vision. Every thought creates cause and effect, good or bad.

We may attempt to cover fear with one excuse after another calling it by different names or blaming it on others like "greed and jealously," *their's* of course. We can even overlook the law of karma and blame God for some wrongdoing we incurred. We often think of hurtful results as punishment. Whatever, fear is the root cause, and fear can bring even a Goliath to his knees.

Clinging and controlling is rooted in fear.
Age grows OLD there.

Fear of Dis-ease

My first teacher of meditation and metaphysics
was an enlightened BEing.
He taught that thoughts are things.
They all teach that you might say, and
while that may be true, still, over
and over he would repeat

Thoughts are things!
Thoughts are things!
Thoughts are things!

One morning I awoke to ten day German measles.
German measles are dangerous for an adult
they can even paralyze you.

On the tenth day I woke up with pain
in every joint of my body
could barely move.
Fear grabbed me.
I rushed to the emergency room.
The doctors shook their heads
"You could have Rheumatoid Arthritis"
they said
"It's a common repercussion."

For the next year I went from one top
Beverly Hills specialist to another.

Although still in my twenties, in their mind
I was doomed for a wheel chair.
Finally, after meditating daily and still
with pain on the rise
I confided in my spiritual teacher.

He looked at me and smiled
" You know . . .
I've had rheumatoid arthritis for 20 years.
Do you see me inhibited in any way
Do you see me in a wheel chair"
?
I was in shock, couldn't believe it!
"It's the *fear* of the disease that cripples
not the disease"
he added.

But my aunt died from rheumatoid arthritis.
It's in my family.
I know how it kills, I insisted.

"The Arthritis was not her death sentence.
IT WAS HER FEAR OF THE DISEASE that killed her.

STOP anticipating pain. Stop thinking in *fear*. Give it up.
It's the *fear* that will cripple you, not the disease."

Copyright © Gabrielle, 02/17/2014

I complied with his advice, and the pains completely disappeared within a month, never to return. Now, at 76 years, I'm trying the same technique with age. Why obsess over a number? Why let a number dictate my health? Why anticipate wrinkles? Why anticipate loss, pain and suffering? Why give in to what I consider, the dark side? Why surrender to fear? Surrender to love instead.

LOVE & MARRIAGE

Statistics prove that most married couples are happier, healthier and live longer. I can remember spending so much of my youth searching for the ONE. Now, I can see that the ONE can only exist in the absolute within ONE'S heart. Since most of us don't realize this, we become more determined to find the ONE outside ourselves, and of course, that is necessary for the growth of humanity; still, we blindly seek only a part of the whole.

Meanwhile, I remember high school in Wichita, Kansas. There were 700 graduates in my class and there was only one guy I could pin as the ONE, and so, when he left me heartbroken for another – I left Kansas. For me, there were no others *out there*. After living in St. Louis, Los Angeles and Hawaii, two marriages and countless possibilities later, I found the part we generally refer to as the ONE. "A match made in heaven!" An astrologer joyfully exclaimed way back in 1985.

According to the Holy Megillah, the Nasarean Bible of the Essene Way . . . divorce was permissible back in ancient times.

Mates could, should and would change with time, often leaving the couple to have nothing in common and nothing to learn from each other. Since every flower is born to reach for the light and grow, our constant search for the ONE may require two, three or even more marriages. No mistake. No shame. No blame. Would a *God of Love* really judge and condemn He/r own cherished offspring?

My quest ended in 1985 when I met my best friend, (12 years younger), who became my best lover and later became my 3rd and final husband. Although he was an entrepreneur of a successful and glamorous travel business, he was, and is an excellent gardener. He cooks better than I do, prepares all our meals and takes excellent care of me . . . like a doll, or his favorite treasure. This fact plus Hawaii's gentle environment and spirit of aloha would have to contribute to my general health, well being and longevity. So . . . thank you God, for blessing me with my Robbie, and thank you for blessing me with the light of Hawaii.

STRESS

"The older I get, the more confused
and afraid I get over the silliest things," she giggled.

"They say" stress is the number one cause of aging. So what do I mean by stress? Stress begins with fear — with trying to get it all done on time and in fear of not BEing or DOing something right according to what "they" think, say and demand. Physically, the aging process is accelerated by a hormone called Cortisol – the higher levels of Cortisol, the faster health deteriorates and signs of age appear. The biggest news is that Cortisol is attracted to stress, and as stress builds to accumulate with time, the body produces more and more Cortisol. This attack on the body is just Cortisol doing it's job. So, if stress is rooted in fear and fear creates worry followed by the age destroyer, Cortisol . . . what good does worry do?

Worry wears and tears to make us
Old before our time . . .

What if I'm not pretty enough, smart enough, good enough? What if I make a mistake? What will *they* think? What if the fire burns my house down? What if I become homeless? What if he doesn't really love me? What if I can't have children? What if Johnny dies? What if I have cancer? Am I too old? And the list goes on and on and on. Watch how this invasion of fearful thoughts slip into a corner of your mind, then watch how fast they multiply to take over your whole body. And that *takeover* — steals your time on Earth, after it steals your youth.

Love patiently abides in quiet aptitude. Fear is in a hurry to rule your conscious and subconscious mind, heart, soul and emotions. *Fear is the enemy* making war wherever you are. A great American president, Franklin D. Roosevelt, once claimed: "There is nothing to fear but fear itself." And if that's true, then of course, your solution is to simply *Let Go of Fear.*

THE ART OF LETTING GO

We've heard so much about *Letting Go*, and *Letting Go* is perhaps one of the greatest keys to finding the *Fountain of Youth,* but who can really *Let Go?* I mean, that is really challenging when you have a lot of baggage, and most anyone past age 40 carries a LOT of baggage.

Once, in a lucid dream, when I knew I was dreaming and came to a part where I had to give all my favorite things away, I exclaimed to the dream characters: "Letting go is SO hard, even in a dream."

Lucid dreams have taught me to see, hear, taste, touch and feel how we are seemingly awake in a dream within dream. Unless the nocturnal dream is lucid, we don't even remember we are asleep — dreaming.   It all seems so real, just like our 3rd dimension feels so real . . . are we easily duped or what?

So what do I mean by "Letting Go?" Well, the opposite of Letting Go is hanging on, often clinging to that which no longer matters, either spiritually, mentally or physically. I would especially advise not to hang on to any limiting beliefs attached to age. Aging in a dream is pure imagination. Are you thinking what I'm thinking?

Letting go of attachments is probably the most important thing we can do to prevent premature aging. And just what does that mean? I always see PREVENT PREMATURE AGING on cream and lotion bottles, tubes and jars in many retail stores and ads. I'm especially skeptical of any claims since I used to write ad copy for such items. Due to mass deception, it was when I saw how writing copy to convince others they needed something they didn't, that I recognized my involvement in an evil art form and walked away. Any form of deception belongs to the innate nature of . . . well, you know who . . .

Now, let's consider the word "attachment." Psychologists look upon the idea as a negative form of caring too much — of clinging to someone or something to the point of addiction. Buddhism looks upon attachment as "Upadana," a cause of suffering, and I'll be the first to agree that to identify with the body is most definitely a major cause of suffering.

I can truthfully admit I started looking in the mirror for wrinkles around my eyes at the tender age of 24, mostly because "they said" that's the age they begin to appear. And who were they? Mostly, they were the ad moguls.

Admittedly embarrassing, I'm still "attached" to my youth and beauty. It's a lot easier to move through the world when you can use your youth as an excuse for any of life's errors, when you can dazzle your friends or foes with the batting of eyelashes, a giggle or a big smile. This brings to mind a poem based on a true story I posted on my Poet's Site a few years ago

Addiction to Vanity

A woman

Can't blame or change the mirror

If she doesn't like what she sees

But she can, and will often

Paint her face

Color her hair

Pluck her brows

Puff her lips and

Pierce her ears to

Alter the reflection

I recall such a friend who

One day answered her door

To an attractive delivery man

With nothing in place

Hair a mess and barefaced

She began to apologize . . . . .

To make excuses for the way she

Appeared

Suddenly, she hurriedly

Ran to a nearby table

Grabbed a gilded framed photo

Of her most glamorous image

Perfectly groomed with the

Painted face

Puffed lips

Coiffed hair

And dangles in her ears

"I don't really look like THIS"

She assured, fluffing disheveled hair

"This is the way I REALLY look!"

She proudly exclaimed, flaunting the

Retouched Photo of a beautiful woman

Perfectly groomed

The attractive man winced

Then grinned, politely, and

As he walked out the door

Her vanity remained

Totally in place

Hungry for attention

Quickly . . .

She ran to her Mirror.

Yes, I really had such a friend and I'll never forgot her story. It taught me that vanity is indeed, a dis-ease — a form of self betrayal — a personal attack on the "True Self" — always feeling less, never feeling good enough, worthy enough, young enough. Maybe the old superstition that to break a mirror makes for seven years bad luck is all wrong. Maybe to break a mirror really offers a big clue, an opportunity to see and recognize yourself as WHOLE in each broken piece without concern of the IMAGE: how it looks, how it performs, how it appears and compares in the world of Maya (illusion). Maybe breaking the mirror is really a lesson in Truth.

So, am "I" vain? Oh yeah, big time vain. It has to be one of my seven deadly sins, if there is such a thing. Youth is obviously rooted in health, general well being, and again, *thinking makes it so.* So the earlier you get started on your awareness of health and longevity, the longer you will "play your part well" on stage, in the light.

> *BEcome like the little child who is busy*
> *living the dream.*

Pseudo Beliefs

Tired, worn and pale
Our natural inheritance of
BLISS
Fades into a long lost mystery like
The Holy Grail.
We focus on our game
We work, and we pray
We struggle and strife to
Preserve and conserve our
Dualistic concerns
Sincerely believing

That's Life!

Goals

"Self-realization is your only purpose for BEing."

I've never been much for setting goals, but there were definite dreams of greatness, which I now recognize as a memory of my true self, BEfore BEginning. Seldom do I dream about getting or becoming anymore, nor do I feel this lack of ambition to be a symptom of old age. Symptoms need not manifest into any form of dis-ease, unless we "think it so," because "they say" that's what happens to OLD people. "Oh, but *they* have proof," you might add . . .

> *"Faith is a knowledge within the heart,*
> *beyond the reach of proof."*
> *--Khalil Gibran*

CREATING BLOBS IN YOUR LIFE?

So what's a blob?

Ordinarily a blob would mean a mark of imperfection. What do I mean by imperfection? The following poem story illustrates a unique and valuable point of view. . .

Beauty of a Blob

Andrea was a best friend
an internationally renowned artist.

I was a bit envious
      and envy isn't really my thing
but I tend to labor over my art
      and she . . .
well, it was the freedom
of her style to just let it flow
      with no effort to control
the paint, or the brush.
      Yes, I envied that.

One day while having coffee
watching Andrea paint
      a big annoying blob
      suddenly
dropped from her brush and
      onto the canvas.

She ignored it
      while I, I continued
to stare at the blob

      appalled by it

      stuck on it
      obsessed with it.
Isn't she going to fix that?
Smooth it over with another color?
Is she just going to leave that big blob?

I wondered — said nothing.

Andrea kept painting.
　　In the time I drank my coffee
she finished her painting.

"Isn't it beautiful?"
　　She asked
　　holding it up for me to see.

"I'm going to call it Balance and Harmony."

Andrea always named her paintings.
The names were part of her art.
　　I couldn't believe
she didn't even seem to notice
　　the blob.

A few months later I attended her exhibit.
　　Like a superstar
Andrea entered the room
　　to the sound of applause.
　　Glancing the gallery walls
I noticed the painting with the blob.
　　Yep, still there
now flaunting itself behind
the glass of an expensive frame
a price tag of $5,000
and a red dot to the side
silently shouting . . .

SOLD

I mused at how I was still hung up
　　on the blob, and how Andrea
had moved on to fill surrounding walls
　　with splendid dancing images.

But that's the way she pictured her life
      Harmony and Balance
were her goals, and in spite
      of all the little or big blobs
uneven lines and textures that splattered
      her canvas of life
Andrea would just let it all go and carry on
as though it really didn't matter
      and in truth, she proved
      it didn't.

Copyright © Gabrielle, 03/21/2011

Are You Creating
the Life of Your Dreams?

The only person you are destined to become
is the person you decide to be.

If you watch TV and the latest hit shows like: THE VOICE, AMERICAN IDOL, RISING STAR and so on, you're familiar with all those young talents talking about fulfilling their dreams. The common thread is: "I've dreamed of this moment my whole life." I smile to myself because their whole life generally equals nine to twenty-something years; yet, they all say the same thing over, and over and over. Bottom line, they are out to prove themselves to the world. They have a gift and want to share it. They want the world to know and appreciate their gift, and them. They have made a decision to be a star, and they are striving to create the life of their dreams.

With or without that special talent, we all want to be acknowledged and appreciated for whatever we do. It's inherent. Deep down we know we are special, because we are. Our talent is never abandoned by the ONE, regardless of our age or condition. We are the ones who give up and abandon our dreams.

It's to be expected that the dreamers, the musical contestants of now, would appear younger and younger as I grow older and older. I wonder if it was always that way and we were ignorant of the fact due to the times and lack of media exposure. Maybe Chopin and Mozart would have been "out there" to the same level and degree had technology been developed to reach across the planet during their time.

Obviously, this popular advancement offers more opportunity to engage in early exposure and competitive recognition. Such opportunities didn't exist in my years of growing up. I recently read where the population has tripled since the fifties which might have something to do with the currant burst of talent.

Do you remember how old you were the first time someone pinched your soft puffy cheeks and asked: "What do you want to BE when you grow up?" And who would really know unless they were one of those who sat in God's front row of volunteers and raised their hand to BE a Beethoven, a Beatle, a Sarah Bernhardt, a Marilyn Monroe or a Steve Jobs?

Even if you were one of those you might just guess at whatever was attracting your attention at the time, be it dolls, a little red fire engine, blocks, balls, and more recently, computer games. And when you grew up, you would aim to excel and strive to meet the demands of those childhood flavors, we call, dreams. Yes, we're back to dreams, the building blocks of ambition, a sense of fulfillment, however long it lasts in this fleeting moment of time.

So what will you BE when soft young cheeks become shriveled and crinkled, when it's all been done and said and you feel quite finished, empty of dream and imaginings in your heart and head? What happens when *they say*, "Game's over. Time to *retire*?"

How will you occupy time left? Maybe you weren't meant to BEcome anything. Maybe you've come to realize the adventure to Earth is like the meaning of a place called Kauai, a little island in Hawaii way out in the middle of the ocean. Kauai, simply means, "Come and BE." Still, what does THAT mean? I recall my first teacher of meditation and metaphysics constantly repeating:

"You cannot BEcome that which you already are;
you can only BE it."
— *Jacques Hondorus*

Since Kauai, Hawaii, is my current home on planet earth, I am particularly mindful as to what it means to simply BE. Does that mean you just go fishing and forget about your creative nature, your desire to BEcome? Or does TO BE mean a state of BEing no different from the child in you, the active, creative child before running to BEcome someone or something — to show the world how rich, talented, smart and special you were, could be, and still are beneath the mask of age? Maybe TO BE means you won't feel a need to PROVE anything anymore, not because you got too old for self discovery, but because you're finally old enough to get a glimpse of the big picture.

One thing for sure, whenever and wherever you are, how you think and feel dictates how you occupy your allotted time on Earth. Recent hot advice created by America's Life Coach, Dr. Ron Jenson, is to "Make a Life, not just a Living."

It's unfortunate to believe that hobbies are just for kids and *old* people. The word hobby is a word we use to disguise the freedom of creativity. According to Wikipedia: A **hobby** is a regular activity that is done for pleasure, typically during one's leisure time. While an amateur may be as skilled as a professional, a professional receives compensation while an amateur generally does not. An amateur simply enjoys the art and act of creativity.

What a blessing when you realize that you are the one to set the rules, deserve the right to enjoy your so-called hobby and accept the opportunity to be grateful.

Reminiscing

It was her 75th birthday.
I come from Happy Days, she smiled.

You know, When Father Knows Best
everything was Small Neat
and Smoke Gets in Your Eyes —

The time of Doo Wop, the Swing
and Elvis, the King of Rock.

Yes, I come from the time of petticoats
bobby sox and saddle shoes, but all that was just
another great disguise, she sighed . . .
Only the costumes, trends and styles
appear to change.

It's always about
Where the Boys Are
Are You Lonesome Tonight
Love Me Tender, and

SMILE

"Smile, though your heart is breaking
Smile, even though it's aching."

SMILE

Copyright © Gabrielle, 2/01/2012

Spread your good cheer and BE Happy,
wherever you are, whatever your age.

I too come from Happy Days. I've lived through some amazing times and discoveries. My generation went from the first commercial air travel with a proper, attentive stewardess to super men called astronauts rocketing to the moon. We went from party lines to the high tech age of wireless international communication. Now, that's gotta count for something. Through all that I have found the SMILE to be one of the most important expressions of all time because . . .

Like LOVE

a Smile is more

CONTAGIOUS

Than any Dis-ease.

The Art of Laughter

We've heard it before: "Laughter is the best medicine, good for the soul. Laughter will keep you young," and it's all true. "They say" that you reincarnate according to your final thoughts. If you die in sorrow, you'll reincarnate to become a sad person, so I figure that if the last thing I do before going to sleep is laugh, and if I die in my sleep, I just might reincarnate to remain bliss-fully happy throughout my future life. Watching sitcoms has become a bedtime routine because sitcoms are so inane, they distract my intellect and make me laugh.

LAUGHTER

Bubbles to Heal.

BE WELL

Smile, and Laugh at it all.

The Art of Gratitude

We hear so much about benefits attached to the art of Gratitude. Truthfully, there is no art to giving thanks but sometimes it's easier to count that which ISN'T, than to be grateful for that which IS.

What do I mean by gratitude? To me, gratitude is a heartfelt, "Thank You." Thank you for my *smile* and the will to shine through all that is and isn't in my life. Years ago, *The Art of Mahikari,* a spiritual practice of giving Divine Light for purpose of spiritual healing, called me to learn the Divine Teachings and help give and spread Divine Light. In nine years of practice which included countless hours of counseling, I learned that all True Light is Divine, and that to freely give without thought of loss or gain, is identical to receiving. One principle guideline for members was to be grateful for absolutely EVERYTHING from morning to night.

EVERYTHING means both good and bad. Even when someone steps on your toes, you say, "thank you." Stepping on toes might erase some negative karma in which case pain would be a good thing, so there are never any bad experiences or bad guys. I realize that may sound somewhat idealistic in theory, but let's not forget how the concept of good and bad are determined by personal perceptions.

Gratitude doesn't require an elaborate speech or mantra for thanking God or the powers that be. I'm reminded of a story told by Jonathan Robinson on Kauai's Community Radio. When Jonathan first began his spiritual journey, he heard of a powerful, secret mantra a master guru in India used for Gratitude.

Jonathan travelled for eighteen hours, over oceans, mountains, hills and valleys in quest of the guru. He even rode in the back of a bumpy truck on a dirt road with a chicken on his lap. When Jonathan finally reached the master he explained he had come all the way from America to learn the secret mantra for gratitude. After some hesitation, the master said: "Since you have come all the way from America, I will tell you." He whispered in his ear . . .

"Thank you"

Needless to say Jonathan was more than disappointed, after all, he had traveled thousands of miles to be told something he already knew. Science concurs that all thoughts cause chemical changes in the brain. Thoughts of gratitude work much like antidepressants bringing on a sense of peace and calmness that would rival the best pharmaceuticals. Gratitude is a constant prayer that promotes a healthy attitude, and a healthy attitude supports the spirit, mind and body as one, but we have to remember to be grateful for absolutely EVERYTHING.

Thank you . . .

for eyes to see your magnificent show

and walk in wondrous majesty

Thank you . . .

for the pain of rejection and insecurity

that I may see more clearly

Thank you . . .

for ears to hear natures constant song

in perfect Harmony

Thank you . . .

for allowing me to hear gossip's blame and

shame that I may feel compassion

Thank you . . .

for nature's rich scent exceeding the

fragrance of rarest perfumes

Thank you . . .

for the stint of enemies who resent my very BEing

that I may learn to forgive them

Thank you . . .

for an open heart that I may receive my inherent

gift of love and share it with others

Thank you . . .

for all my fear and resentment

that I may grow to overcome all inadequacies

THANK YOU for all this and even more

The Art of Attitude

Attitude reflects a form of Gratitude in action.

What do I mean by Attitude? Attitude isn't a form of arrogance or posturing, but it is a form of true confidence reflected in every move you make. Posture and movement are the first reflections of your attitude. Do you sit, stand and walk with head held high, straight and tall, or do you slump and shuffle?

Posture demonstrates a lot about how you feel physically and mentally. If you are feeling good about yourself and moving forward, growing young with vitality, your back is straight and you walk and sit with pride. There are basically two reasons we slump: we are either in pain, or we're too lazy to sit and stand straight. It's so much easier to slump because, let's face it, sitting and standing straight takes a lot of energy.

The habit of slumping can, and often does begin during teen years. Slumping at that early age forms the muscles of your future. It's the first visible sign of aging long before your time, in addition, there are proven medical benefits for organs when standing and sitting straight regardless of age.

WHAT DO I MEAN
BY KEEPING THE ENERGY HIGH?

Look Up . . .

One day I sat on a bench across from Starbucks at a local shopping center. I had paused from my busy day to stare at the clouds. There is great inspiration in their effortless, timeless dance. While sipping my coffee, I observed that on this particular day the clouds had gathered to perform an exceptional dance in form and motion. The whole performance was so exciting I wanted to share. Gazing at the shoppers passing by, it was sad to see the majority looking down, staring at the ground as if laboriously carrying all the problems of the whole world in a big bag they had just purchased from a store at the center.

Destiny of a Cloud

Have you ever thought how clouds
Don't think of where to go?

They just float and flow
Wherever the breath
Of breeze may
Blow

Clouds don't worry
How long they will last
What they will become and how fast

In a matter of seconds, endless images

61

Can appear to disappear as a lamb, a fish
A dog, a cat, a man puckered with big fat lips
Reaching to kiss a puff of mist

Clouds have great purpose
In merging to separate
Becoming to BE
Dissolving into
Nothing
No where
Gathering thick and dark
Till falling from the heavens

In a final disguise as drops of dew or rain
To nourish and sustain one Heaven on Earth

No, clouds don't care how they change
How their colors paint the sky
Who's looking or how they appear
To human eyes

Clouds just move from
One misty dream to the next
Over land and sea
Day after day
Long through
Night
Totally willing
Totally free

Oh, that I

Might rise to

BE

Like a cloud

HEALTH

A Mother's Tragic Claim

She arrived at the headquarters

of a private rescue center for the abused

tired, worn and disheveled

Her exquisite features

shown beneath a prematurely aged

face and body

marred

scarred

I was once very beautiful, happy and wealthy

she began

lavished with all the riches ever dreamed

but as my children came

my life began to change

Perhaps I spoiled them, but surely
I can't be to blame
They are rude, disrespectful, arrogant
selfish, thoughtless, greedy and cruel

My children have no shame
Even with all my assets
I could not save myself from their abuse
My own flesh and blood!
She exclaimed

In my giving spirit, they ravaged my lands
for their profits and gains
trashed my mansions
stole my precious jewels, rich oils, perfumes
and artful creations from around the world

They consumed and consumed
like it was never enough
fighting bloody battles over
my treasures like animals in prey

My gifts were there for all to share
but they just couldn't see it my way
They chose to disobey my rules
for long, healthy and prosperous lives
scoffed at my wisdom of natural laws —
broke into my savings in name of borrowing
for their cause
never to replenish as promised, depriving
future generations without pause

I kept thinking they would grow to change

find the key to happiness in caring and sharing

but after all these years, my reserves rapidly diminish

I have no choice

I am spent

Finished

God only knows how I've tried!

I hereby state my claim to change my will

she cried

flooding the space with tears of sorrow's rain

I understand madam, said the concerned counselor

This appears to be a universal problem

And your location and name?

EARTH

I AM Mother Earth

The Breath of Life

We can live without food for approximately 40 days.
Depending on the environment, we can live without
water from 2 -7 days, but we can only live
without breath for around 3 minutes.

Keeping the above facts in mind, we might agree that there is more to breathing than an automatic process of inhaling and exhaling. This brings to mind all that we take for granted and literally forget to even whisper a simple "thank you." Let's face it, health like life itself, is a multi-dimensional subject of many theories and beliefs, yet, no one can deny life on Earth begins with the first breath.

I've learned that breath is the one basic thing we all have in common, the one thing that connects us all to the same source. Typically, there are no special vacuums, tubes or arrangements. We all breathe the same air wherever we are. The rich man breathes the same air as the pauper: the master, the disciple, the celebrity, their fans and all those watching, laughing, crying, sharing.

Regardless of your belief system, it's important to realize that breathing deep with conscious awareness is a prerequisite to longevity, health and abundance. The Yogi's have an exercise called the "Breath of Fire" which places emphasis on renewing and ridding the body of disease. I strongly suggest looking into it.

Water

The late, Masaru Emoto, was famous for using water to prove the power of frequency in each expressed thought. Emoto showed the world how within seconds words of love and peace expressed over water formed beautiful crystals, while destructive words of anger, hate and disdain created disfigured or broken non-crystalline forms.

"Water is the mirror that has the ability to show us what we cannot see. It is a blueprint for our reality, which can change with a single, positive thought. All it takes is faith, if you're open to it."

The quote above is from Masaru Emoto's web site. Please check it out for numerous pictures exemplifying his profound discoveries along with more valuable information.

Most of us grew up hearing about the importance of drinking water. I never really took drinking water seriously until moving to Hawaii. I couldn't help but notice how even a dying plant is revived when watered. If water proves so important to the growth, health, beauty and well being of Mother Nature, wouldn't the magic of water apply equally to Human Nature? We do know that Human Nature is generally made up of approximately 70-80% water. It becomes obvious we need to constantly replenish the loss of daily fluid lest body cells become dry, the skin wrinkled, and major organs shrivel to suffer the most results. The heart and brain react immediately due to a lack of oxygen caused by the thickening of blood.

Less water, less oxygen; less oxygen, thicker blood. It makes total sense that thick blood will make the heart work harder to pump through the body. Any amount or form of poison is a NO NO, so please avoid drinking water from toxic, plastic bottles.

We might look at the weeds of earth as unwanted, invaders, much like we acknowledge "germs" as invaders of the human form. Nature is wild and uncontrollable. Give nature a space and she will fill it. If we don't fill it with what she needs, then look out for germs and weeds, for surely they are ready to take over. So water a plant with love and watch it thrive. Don't forget, even a plant has a destined full cycle, and does not the blossom of a plant return the following season? So can we agree that nature in whatever form needs water for growth, to blossom, thrive and drop seed for a new generation?

Diet

Unfortunately Kauai, Hawaii, is home and testing ground for GMO food products. No, I would never have made Kauai my home had I known these toxic invaders would appear. Recent reports by *Cascadia Times* have further revealed the exceptional volume of highly toxic pesticides being used in Hawaii by such corporations as Monsanto, DuPont, Pioneer, Syngenta, Dow and BASF often adjacent to communities and sensitive environmental areas.

"The four transnational agribusinesses that are experimenting with genetically engineered crops on Kauai have transformed part of the island into one of the most toxic chemical environments in all of American agriculture." So, how do GMO foods come about?

"Genetically modified organisms, or GMOs, are created when a gene from one species is transferred to another, creating something that would not be found in nature."
— *Mark Bittman.*

TAKE HEED

Of this engineered

One time sterile seed.

Why partake of

Food sprayed

With lethal

Combinations of

Chemical Solutions

Designed to stunt all

Reproductive evolution?

GMO

Poison to the core

Yet, disguised in glory

On the shelves of your

Grocery Store.

Below is a direct quote from an article on the Internet titled:

"What Foods are GMO's in?"

"It is estimated that GMOs are in 70% or more of the processed foods on grocery store shelves. Commercial production of GMO corn, soybeans, canola and papayas has been approved by the FDA and at least one of those crops are in a large percentage of processed foods. They are not labeled as GMO. The HFCS (high fructose corn syrup) in most soft drinks in the United States very likely comes from GMO corn.

"Products that have soy in them, including soy milk, are likely to have GMOs in them. Meats and dairy products on grocery store shelves, including beef, pork, turkey, chicken, processed meats, etc. are likely to have come from factory - farmed animals using rBGH hormone.

What is rBGH? **Recombinant Bovine Growth Hormone** is a genetically engineered copy of a naturally occurring **hormone** produced by cows, manufactured by Monsanto Company."

This section on Health is not intended to play war games with the chemical corporations, so I will say no more and encourage you to please find additional information on your own. Everything you need to know is available on line. You will learn the difference between GMO crops, traditionally grown farming and organic foods. The danger of Pesticides have raced to the headlines of GMO crops. PLEASE make yourself aware of what is on your dinner plate.

Since no two bodies are alike, I can't really say a particular diet is good for you because it appears good for me. It's important to take location into consideration. A New Yorker won't have the same choice, or even need of certain foods as I do living in Hawaii, so again, since this is not a "How To" book, please allow me to speak only for myself. Considering the general health of Mother Earth: her depletion of minerals, polluted air and seas, loss of trees and oxygen, poisoned lands and pseudo natural foods we can no longer just take it all for granted. Personal research becomes obvious – well worth the time and effort to become aware of your diet, surroundings, and what you are asking your body to digest.

Supplements Anyone?

Do we need them? Since we depend on Earth for our daily

food and sustenance, it's simply logical that we can only be as healthy as our Earth is healthy. Considering Mother Earth's declining condition, it's safe to say we need supplements. It's best to consult a licensed nutritionist for individual needs. In addition, the only way to know what is BEST for YOU is to study your body, beginning with your thoughts, belief systems, physical signs and ailments. Be sure to make every effort to read labels and eat organic whenever possible.

"They say" organic is too expensive, but how valuable is your health? Would you rather spend money on pure foods and supplements now, or on doctor bills later?

> *When the Dalai Lama was asked*
> *what surprised him most about humanity, he said:*
> *"Man, because he sacrifices his health in order to*
> *make money. Then, he sacrifices money*
> *to recuperate his health."*

Some may argue that many parents can't really afford to even think of what foods are best for their family. They feel blessed to have any food to put on the table, even having a table to put it on could be considered fortunate.

For those, my heart goes out to you. It's not good for anyone to consume food that contains even a small dose of daily poison. Poison accumulates to spread through the body until ...

To date, I take no medication. I consult with Naturopathic and Ayurvedic doctors regarding any signs of aliments, find more benefits from thermography as opposed to mammograms, have a medical examination and blood tests once a year and always study food contents. Bottom line — I don't do medicine with exception of emergencies, which are fortunately very few. Although I have great respect for the medical association (my mother was a registered nurse) and medicine, which certainly has its place, I find that most medication masks pain and symptoms allowing the root *cause* of any symptom to continue to flourish, spread, and eventually kill the body. We can't cure the *cause* with medicine, but we can cure the cause *naturally.* Unfortunately, that experience can take a painful, yet necessary amount of time while leading back to the benefits of health.

TV commercials are right to provide information as to how one medication begets another, and taking even one can kill you. You've just got to love the fact they end with contact information for an attorney in case your loved one dies, becomes paralyzed and so on . . . Hellllllllooooo — are you paying attention? Remember the time when TV didn't allow any commercials for lingerie, medicine, doctors or attorneys?

Maintaining a level of weight is important for heart and general well being. Consider that every extra ten pounds of weight is like strapping a ten pound bucket of sand to your back. Of course, you are never able to put it down. Now that's a HEAVY and laborious thought.

As for sweets, I make every effort to avoid the temptation, but I do slip from time to time. It is best to always avoid any food product with *High Fructose Corn Syrup,* and processed sugar in general.

Eating out is a bit risky these days; you just don't know where the restaurant of choice purchased the food on your plate, or exactly how it was prepared and by whom, but hey, don't become a fanatic. Any form of fanaticism is a sign of imbalance, and don't forget, balance is one of our greatest challenges on this tightrope of life.

Exercise

Lots of books have been written about the importance of diet and exercise, so we all know to take the time to indulge in these conscious acts towards health and well being, especially as we age, lest we regress to wobble like a toddler.

Here again, follow the rhythms of your body. Follow the direction that is right for you, that meets YOUR physical needs. At 43 years of age I awoke to the fact I had been physically coasting. I realized a conscious diet wasn't enough, that the blessing of a healthy body wouldn't last long without the assistance of some form of exercise. I became an Ashtanga Yogi for three years. The exercise was impossible without breathing into the postures. Breath was and is also a major key to tuning into the Divine. The dance was perfect for me at the time, but due to the physical intensity, Ashtanga Yoga is not for everyone.

The physical form of Yoga does happen to be a foundation for unity of body, mind and spirit which makes Yoga my preference; fortunately, there are a number of Yogic choices. Tai Chi is my second choice, but the gym may be yours, and that's good too. Dance is always an awesome way to keep the body moving, and a brisk walk in the fresh air is totally invigorating. The important thing to remember is to breathe deep, keep moving and celebrate being alive.

*We don't get old and stiff because
our body gets tired of moving; we get old
and stiff because we stop moving.*

Going to Starbucks is always a treat because the ambiance is so lively, full of people still running on the edge of time, still climbing the mountain in quest of fulfillment. Along my way, I've learned it's not the climb that steals your zest for life, it's the disappointments along the way. Exercise contributes to revise and ignite your zest. Keep climbing.

Ah, but to Sleep . . .

Okay, so you realize the importance of sleep. Nothing works right if you don't get enough sleep, and sleepless nights are effecting everyone, everywhere. Sleep deprivation reaches an all time high creating new insomniacs from teens on. There are way too many to count. Maybe you no longer jump up like a kid excited to start your day. You now know what the day could bring, and maybe, just maybe it's not all that, so you want to go back to sleep the moment you open your eyes. You get up because you're supposed to. You drag yourself through your day and struggle to keep up with conversations. You might think all this is just a normal part of aging. Nothing could be further from the truth. A registered nurse with savvy and curiosity, Mother explained the importance of sleep very much like . . .

The Harvard Women's Health Watch suggests six reasons to get enough sleep:

1. *Learning and memory: Sleep helps the brain commit new information to memory through a process called memory consolidation.*

2. *Metabolism and weight: Chronic sleep deprivation may cause weight gain by affecting the way our bodies process and store carbohydrates, and by altering levels of hormones that affect our appetite.*

3. *Safety: Sleep debt contributes to a greater tendency to fall asleep during the daytime. These lapses may cause falls and mistakes such as, air traffic and road accidents.*

4. *Mood: Sleep loss may result in irritability, impatience, inability to concentrate, and moodiness. Too little sleep can also leave you too tired to do the things you like to do.*

5. *Cardiovascular health: Serious sleep disorders have been linked to hypertension, increased stress hormone levels, and irregular heartbeat.*

6. *Disease: Sleep deprivation alters immune function, including the activity of the body's killer cells. Keeping up with sleep may also help fight cancer.*

The Night Sweeps Me Away

Shrouded in mystery

Each night

~ I Die ~

I die to the light of day as

Darkness sweeps me away

To escape in dreams

No one else can see.

I travel to unknown places

And meet with people

I seem to know

Feel love and fear

Pleasure and pain.

Nothing has really changed

From day dream to nocturnal

And then

In the morning light

I Die

I die to the dream

Of the darkened night.

But where did all those places

And all those people come from

And where did they go?

Just what Am I to them

Now?

Are we buried

In each other's mind

As one and the same, or

Within the ground of

Dreamscape

In another place

Another time?

It matters not.

I am alive

To begin anew

Here, now, in the light

Until the night comes

To sweep me away

And I die ~

I die

To another day.

Each time we close our eyes to sleep,

we face unknown territories. How can we be sure

we will ever return from our adventure into darkness?

Were we really afraid to die, would we not be afraid to sleep?

Instead, we often run to sleep to escape life's demands.

So what are we really afraid of: life or death?

And does sleep not prove life and death

variables of one and the same illusion

with eyes wide open to day ~

closed tight by night?

The View

It appears that after we reach a certain stage in life we "get" enough of a view to see beyond all that "getting it together" stuff. From my point of view, the most important thing to remember is not to be seen as a hopeless, mature soul, one that will generally slip into a costume of "old" and adjust to the style.

Clinging to old ideas of self can become a huge burden if obsessed with . . .

APPEARANCE

How Do I Look . . . ?
Too skinny, too fat, too wrinkled, too OLD?

My Mask is Missing

Oh, where have I put it?
Perhaps I left it on the plane
On the bus
On the beach
Or drifting in fields of dust
Or did I drop it in the streets
On the road
Somewhere near my home
Away from me
Away from you
Away from us?

My mask is missing
I'm naked now
Naked to the core
Disguised no more
Can't hide
Can't pretend
Now they'll see
I'm just like
Them.

Funny how we always want to be the same as everyone else till we reach the age when we see that to be like everyone else is well . . . the same. It's when we realize that to be ourself is a good thing, and all it takes to be different is to simply and completely be ourself.

In our quest to reveal our most unique and attractive self, we often run to make-up and costumes. Personally, I love to costume. I do tend to call clothes "costumes" because through every stage of growth, and every trend and style, we change clothes like costumes in a play. Since my career began with fashion, I can't deny my continued love of design, color and style.

As for men, other than covering their bodies with tattoos, men's fashions don't really count. I mean, women are sporting an equal number of tattoos, piercings and all those same, primal fashion statements, but year after year, men's fashion appears similar in style. Though seasonal colors and textures change, and a collar and lapel may move from skinny to fat and back to skinny, like a pant leg can alter from slim to baggy, baggy to slim and all that's in between, for the most part, a guy wears a shirt, pants, a coat and tie.

But women are a totally different breed; a woman is always reinventing herself. Since the 1940's, women have strutted the cat walk wearing not only skirts and gowns of varied length and styles but pants as well — including the expensive, yet shredded, holy jeans of today. Fashion experts aren't exactly clear about what an elder woman should wear, nor do they seem to care what image she presents to the world now that she is cool as opposed to hot.

The fashion world simply reflects the thinking of the young "hotties"— mostly in size *small,* even though statistics reveal the elder population is rising to the majority. Although we are clearly not our bodies, did you stop caring how you look? I didn't. To me, costuming is just another form of art, part of BEing a total statement.

Face Painting

As for the cosmetic counter — in general, I do love cosmetics. I've never been attracted to a theatrical application, but I do find that every woman benefits from a hint of color. If we are willing to indulge in decorating our face and bodies with permanent ink what's wrong with a touch of temporary color on the cheeks, lips and eyes?

Beware of logo claims. I'm always offended by the 20 year old models supposedly looking younger with the aid of the featured cosmetic. It would be far more convincing to use mature models to demonstrate the product's validity.

So, have I had cosmetic surgery, Botox, face peels and/or other harsh remedies? NO. Oh, I will admit to an occasional purchase of Lancome or Estee Lauder to get that free bag of samples at Macy's, but truthfully, I have never found any of the little samples more beneficial than any natural lines purchased at drug or health food stores, preferably, paraben-free products.

For me, cosmetics and dressing the part began on the morning of my 8th grade graduation. I was so excited. Finally I could pretend to *be* grown up. Finally, I was a beautiful swan ready for a bigger and better pond. The next year I would walk the halls of Saint Mary's High. So, in celebration of my graduation I wore my first high heeled shoes. They were white to match my dress, and I painted my lips the prettiest pink. When entering my 8th grade room at Blessed Sacrament Intermediary, all heads turned.

Sister Isadora immediately grabbed my arm in utter disgust. Her thin, pale lips grimaced tighter than ever as she roughly led me down the hall, and into the little girls' room. She placed me before a long mirror with numerous classmates — primping. Sister Isadora sternly ordered: "Now, just look at yourself." I did, and thought I looked really pretty with my new pink lips in spite of the fact I was ready to cry over Sister Isadora's reaction. But that wasn't all, she then handed me a tissue and harshly demanded . . .

"Now, wipe that paste off your lips."

Although totally humiliated in front of my young, gossipy competitors, I was determined not to drench myself in tears before racing down the long hall and back to my classroom with Sister Isadora still tugging at my arm. A red, crying face could ruin everything and accomplish nothing. I was determined to be pretty — as I thought and felt pretty to be at the time. So, I quietly obeyed Sister Isadora and wiped that paste off my lips.

Over the years, away from Sister Isadora's strict watch, I would purchase "paste" of many colors and wonder why it always looked so much more promising in the tube than on my lips. Every color purchased was invariably too red or too pink, too pale or too dark — always suggesting I needed something more or something less. To this day, I have yet to find the perfect color and texture.

Truthfully, there are no two days we look the same, feel the same, are the same. With every thought, each moment brings a new you, and each decade takes that statement to a completely different level.

Having nothing to do with age, even our skin tone changes with the lighting, what we had for dinner the night before, how we slept, and how well we are handling the challenges of our new day. Most importantly, are we following our path of Love or of Fear? Are we remembering to breathe?

In the middle of all those attempts to appear perfectly beautiful, to meet critical worldly demands and expectations, we forget our mission to go back, back *BEfore BEginning.* We are so consumed by society and it's media blitz to glamorize all the distractions, it's easy to forget.

Oh, and how times have changed! Some parents now give their young daughters' breast implants for high school graduation. Celebs as early as 30 and sometimes younger, run to Botox in their race against time to compete with the new, rising stars — all those young girls and women still outwardly searching for "the one," justifiably indulging in their revolving quest around the chemistry of hormones. It appears that when sexual hormones are no longer running the show, calling a physical mate, a career, a will to "make it" and dress the part of HOT, the show is over. Done. Finis. The End.

Sun Love . . .

"Stay out of that old sun," Mother used to insist. Mother had beautiful porcelain skin until she left the planet at age 84. She creamed her face in a nightly ritual for at least 30 minutes, and she avoided the sun like the plague. It wasn't until moving to Hawaii at age 39 that I indulged in a suntan. Hawaii, forever warm, always calls for exposed skin as opposed to fashionable coverings.

I baked in the sun on the beach nearly everyday for fourteen years, and never looked or felt better. It was when moving to Big Island that everything changed. It was just a natural progression of turning back to white, which does tend to age me more than sun bronzing.

Truthfully, I would never indulge in a tanning booth for all the obvious reasons. Happily, I recently read where morning sun is actually good for you. You may be aware that vitamin D is one of the body's necessary requirements. While the sun naturally emits vitamin D and contains lots of nourishment for internal body parts, morning sun won't burn the skin. Contrary to popular belief, tanning isn't really a sign of health, but the body's way of protecting itself from the sun.

ACT 111

THE SENIOR MOMENT

If life is a classroom, like "they say" —
a place of constant lessons, then our education
must provide one clue after another, in which case
one of the most threatening clues to aging would be
The Senior Moment.

If old enough, please strike the words: "I'm having a Senior Moment" from your vocabulary. To me, it's like saying you *retired.* When a ten year old claims he forgot his homework, his cell phone, his back pack, his lunch money, do we exclaim "OMG! He's having a *Senior Moment?"* No. We scream . . .

"What do you mean you forgot your homework?"

I'm not talking about the disease, Alzheimers; I'm talking about forgetting things like keys, and someone's name. If we buy the theory that we're getting the dreaded disease when we can't remember simple things, then we'll surely get it — and if we agree to the whole package, we'll get that too with no refunds.

I remember a time when my home town had a movie theater or two, and going to the movies was a weekend treat. Television and the Internet had yet to be, so, it was easy to remember movies and actors. Now, with over 1,000 TV networks, on line information, hundreds of daily emails, and thousands of movie theaters across the planet, has it ever occurred to you that the older you get the more you have to remember? So, naturally, you would forget things like the name of an actor who played in — what was the name of that movie? In addition, we could all be suffering from information overload.

And what about all those times in younger years when we got stuck on a name or something we couldn't remember? Then we had the line: "Oh, his name is right on the tip of my tongue." We didn't call those *Senior Moments* because we were young, only twenty or thirty something.

In fact, science has discovered we have 100 billion brain cells. In our late 20s to early 30s our brain looses volume, the cortex becomes thinner, the myelin sheath surrounding the fibers of our neurons begins to degrade, and the brain receptors don't fire as quickly. During our 30s, memory begins to slip as the number of neurons in the brain decreases. It may take longer to learn new things or memorize words or names. This process continues in the decades ahead, putting many in a constant state of thinking: "OMG! I'm on my way to Alzheimers."

Scientists have long believed that by early adulthood the brain has solidified and little plasticity can be expected afterwards. What if that point of view is an old paradigm — like when "they" believed the world was flat and sailing the seas of space to the moon was an impossible dream? Again, I am reminded of spirit first, mind subordinate and body follows. Be sure to read: *You are the Placebo,* by Dr. Joe Dispenza.

This might appear to be a form of denial, but it's really a form of choosing a new reality, a form of *Keeping the Energy High.* Remember, the fleeting moment is a permanent endowment.

I feel as though something is missing in my life . . .

I once whined to a well-known channel
from the Mount Shasta area.

> *You're absolutely right,* he replied.
> *Oh good, you see that too.*
> *So what's my problem?*
> *What am I missing?*
> *Do you know?*
> *Will you tell me?*

He smiled all knowingly, and responded with
an answer I never expected.

> *YOU are missing.*
> *You are either preoccupied with your past or*
> *reading into the future.*

You are seldom present with the moment, the only time you're ever really alive.

"The Only Time You're Ever Really Alive"

How many times need we hear those words
before we remember to live in the
present moment of . . .

Eternity

pouring forth from the
Fountain of Truth, forever young?
Indivisible threads of the past lace a visible
present into a future dream of constant seem
from moment to moment

Forever Now

If living in the present is to live in eternity, then surely we must turn to truth, the whole truth, and if it's true that we cannot become that which we already are, then there is nothing to seek and nothing to find. You are the *Fountain of Truth.* I am the *Fountain of Truth.* We are the *Fountain of Truth, "and the Truth shall set you free."* Finally we realize . . .

Truth is

Infinite love

In the duality of all

That exists

Everything else

F

A

L

L

S

Under the spell of illusion

Artfully contrived

To distract us

from the

~ Truth ~

TRUTH IS: Copyright © Gabrielle, 04/26/2011

A form of keeping the energy high includes avoiding all those funnies on the internet, funnies that illustrate Barbie as a fat old woman since turning 50 — along with Wonder Woman, Superman, Spiderman, and the whole gang of former superheroes. Avoid any old people jokes promoting old age as forgetful, silly, pathetic and decrepit. Why allow yourself to identify with any of those old paradigms of age? Truthfully, I find them offensive. Remember — "Thinking Makes It So." Picture what you want, express and feel your gratitude even before the image manifests in 3D and living color. FEELING gratitude as you envision your dream as though it has already happened is the one, deep dark *Secret to Manifestation.*

All around the globe we speak of hope for tomorrow. We look to the horizon for a new dawn rising, and while the sun appears to rise in Hawaii, in England, the dawn has come to go — today is almost over. The idea of a rising and setting sun is one of life's great illusions. It took centuries for us to realize that the sun doesn't revolve around us, that it is Earth in her constant state of revolving that rotates to greet the sun — then consistently falls to reflect the moon which moves the tide of seas, and so the cycle repeats over and over as poets and romantics write about the beauty of a rising and setting sun.

Killing Time

How many times have you used the expression:
"I'm just killing time"?

If you agree that time is precious, why kill it? Remember how long it took to get to your first double digit, ten? It seemed to take forever, and after that, remember how the years just seemed to fly? Before you knew it college was over, and then your own kids were graduating from college, and now, "they say" you are old. So why KILL TIME? Best be careful what you say. Time is listening, and before you know it, your time will die away. After all, you've been killing it. Most Masters of the Far East claim that time is strictly a man made concept. I tend to agree, but whatever, please don't attempt to KILL time, instead, BE grateful for time, manmade or not. Don't forget, GRATITUDE reflects a spirit of youth.

As Time Marches On . . .

Sitting in a coffee shop with an old friend from high school –

I never thought what turning 70 would BE like, she sighed, *how I would look, act and feel.*

You don't think about those things at 10, 20, 30 or even 40 years of age. You only dream, and project what you plan to become on a seemingly long, long journey ahead. You think it will last forever, she lamented, observing aged hands.

First, life is all about the present, she sighed again, *there's so much to discover, to see and do, then sadly, when you reach a certain age, life is all about the past.*

You failed to recognize the spontaneity and enthusiasm expressed by the whole being of your once, uncluttered mind, way back then, around the age of three, or even two when you were so young and 'it' was all so new.

As soon as the field of mind becomes clouded with earthy things — distracted by older kids, competition and all those possibilities, it is then — then we begin to plot and plan losing our origin of truth. It is then, fear moves in . . . .

Her voice trailed, and she paused to sip her coffee.

They Say . . .

We mellow with time, and that's a good thing. I watched my father, whom I often referred to as a saint, mellow from a spirited and often temperamental young man to a calm, understanding elder, yet he died of heart failure at age 62, only to return after pronounced dead for a full ten minutes.

He told me there was no other side. This was strange coming from a staunch Catholic who had always believed in heaven, purgatory and hell. "Baby, everything was black," he said, "if they hadn't brought me back I would never have known I had died. I wouldn't have even known I had lived." And then he lived for another fourteen years to heal his broken heart and find peace.

I don't think my father continued to grow once he "retired" at 64. He just sort of drifted from day to day without the challenge of life at a job with co-workers. People need people. People need community, the feeling of belonging and contributing something over and above immediate family. It appeared Daddy was just Killing Time — unconsciously waiting for the end. Again . . .

"Self-realization is your only purpose for BEing."

I've noticed a lot of elders get cranky with age. In addition to physical dis-ease, it appears that all the toxins created out of fear and disappointment collect to linger and disturb most hearts and minds. All feelings of failure to live up to the expectations they had of themselves kind of swallow them up and eat away at them. Even those who have risen to the heights of super star status like Michael Jackson, feel a sense of failure and unfulfilled desire.

Michael Jackson's doctor was recently interviewed on CNN. The host played a recording from a time when Michael was speaking slurred and so slow he was barely comprehensible. His doctor quickly stated we were listening to a man falling asleep. Really? The point is what Michael said in total slow motion: "I want the world to recognize me as the greatest performer in the world." Of course, we, the audience, can rightfully raise our voice to say . . . "OMG, he wanted to be the best, the most and the greatest, but he already was. Didn't he know that?"

So the irony of the story is that Michael Jackson was a Divine being, born with a talent and opportunity that would elevate him from early on to be one of the greatest entertainers in the world, but deep within, he knew he was more, so he worked *overtime* to prove himself to the point it killed him. Michael died a mystery to himself and to us as a result. The really sad part is that beneath the skin of our own disguise, we are all more. We are all Divine, and few know it. Do you know who you really are beneath your great disguise?

Can't help but wonder why we would feel
LESS
than who we are and
MORE
than what we have become.

Age is Relative . . .

Those numbers will get you every time –
if you let them.

It was a summer day in the mid West of Wichita, Kansas when Mother decided to take me for a little walk. Mother was probably in her late twenties and I was a curious three year old. I remember the pavement — grey, with large cracks, hot and close to my face. All was good till Mother stopped to talk to a friend. I quickly grabbed her skirt to hide behind as she and her lady friend exchanged polite greetings. Mother's friend scared me, terrified me. She was too old, and I was afraid of OLD people.

In parting Mother immediately asked, "Why did you hide from Stephanie? She is such a lovely young lady." "Because," I articulated in my three year old voice, "she's too OLD." "Baby," mother responded, kindly, but shocked, "Stephanie's just a young girl; she's only eighteen." Funny, how seemingly insignificant little moments like this can become lifetime lessons.

When my ten year old grandson came to visit me in Hawaii, I showed him my old engagement picture in a yellowed newspaper. The picture was one of four, large enough to occupy a whole page. I was sure he'd be impressed with the large, glamorous picture. He glanced at the page and immediately exclaimed, "Nana, you were so OLD!" My son and I were stunned by the comment. "Son, better watch your words, you'll be that old in another ten years."

EXPECTATIONS

When going to the mirror,
I always expect to look better than the day before.

Does this concept work? For me it does. I don't look for more lines in my face, but for the ones from yesterday to have disappeared after a good night's sleep. Normally, I don't advocate expectations. I tend to find them extremely dangerous — they most always set you up for a big fall, sometimes literally. I recall a night at the University of Kansas, the evening I was to be pinned by my collage sweetheart, my first love.

Since watching the movie *Gone With the Wind*, I had imagined the moment when I would descend from a staircase with the love of my life waiting at the foot of the stairs. His expression would exemplify total intoxication with my beauty and his desire, just like Rhett Butler waiting for Scarlett Ohara to descend Hollywood's version of a magnificent and memorable staircase.

I was wearing a fluffy pink, Christian Dior dress loaned by my rich and fashionable, future mother-in-law. After a few steps down, I tripped and tumbled all the way down to my true love's feet, and yes, ripped the famous designer dress. Although the rip tore in an inconspicuous place, the fantasy, my first expectation of the evening had turned out to be a disaster. I clung to the disappointment of that expectation throughout the entire evening, therefore, all other hopeful expectations of the event, fell.

Way back then, the universe was displaying the downfall of expectations, but I had to experience MORE of the same in a different costume, time and setting to finally, "get it." Call this concept the law of cause and effect, or karma, but what you call it matters not. The law will, and does play itself out as one of our greatest teachers.

"We attract unto ourselves the exact equivalent
of that which we express."
— *Jacques Honduras*

Expect What, When?

When fear rules the heart
you can expect despair.

When insanity rules the heart
you can expect implosion.

When forgiveness rules the heart
you can expect compassion.

When love rules the heart
you can expect miracles.

Copyright © Gabrielle, 03/18/2011

I don't think I look young for my age
I think most other people look old for theirs.

I've been advised not to say that. I'm told that most would be insulted, but what if it's my truth? Our body, the temple of the living spirit, requires constant care. We've established that the outside reflects the condition of the inside: our thoughts, health, energy, and general attitude are revealed in every line, every muscle, every expression and every trip to the doctor. No matter to what extremes we go to cover up our fear, loneliness, disappointment, exuberance and even love for another, is all reflected in the mirror, be it made of glass, water, or the eyes of others.

According to Wikipedia, the online free encyclopedia, the national life expectancy is 79.9 years. This could mean — my act is almost over. From another point of view, didn't people once live to be hundreds of years old? Didn't the biblical Sarah, birth a child at age 90? Many may argue that the gauge of time was different back then; maybe true, maybe not. I wonder why we seem to accept most "hear says" as the whole truth and faithfully adopt such beliefs as our own.

WHAT DO I MEAN
BY KEEPING THE ENERGY HIGH?

The Mystery of Duality

Duality can seem sweet
If mixed just right
Blending the dark with the light
Yet in the eyes of those who realize

The dream of duality is far from
Bliss and Reality
Time to
WAKE UP!
Game's' over
YOU'RE ON!
Don't give up
Till you're
IN

In reality, energy has no in or out. The personal form appears to have an in and an out, so there IS always someplace to go or BE, but the 'real us' is impersonal, and the impersonal self has no defining entrance or exit.

It's kinda like we are not our house. Our house has an in and an out with a front door and a back. In spirit, there is no entrance or exit. In spirit, there is no coming and going. In spirit, we are always home.

In Earth's domain we renovate our house; we decorate and embellish it with our treasures: some sentimental like family heirlooms, some for comfort and some for show. Still, our house only represents our stage. Whatever we do or don't do to our space, whatever props we collect only reflect our character, the part we play in life — the way we think, move and share our BEing. Even so, we don't get that, and so many of us try to create a space of perfection, because perfection dwells deep within, calling all. Unfortunately most fail to really listen and therefore, comprehend the message clearly — we fail to focus on balancing the physical, mental and spiritual needs. How else can we effectively walk the tightrope of life without tripping to fall?

Due to the physical and mental limitations of our society, we somehow think to answer the call of perfection means we have to spend a lot of money. In that way, showing and telling can be very expensive, and so money becomes the focus of our attention, especially when growing our family.

We get lost in the task of acquiring and collecting to prove our self worth. We are driven to "get" a lot of stuff, to play with the biggest and best toys. In later years when the family is grown and the burden gets too heavy, we let it all go, just like little girls let their dolls go and little boys their toy cars. They don't struggle or sacrifice to give them up, they just outgrow the need for them. Funny how that works. Somehow though, we continue to play games throughout our entire life.

When we were school children, most of us hated homework. We hated answering to our parents and school authorities. We could hardly wait to grow up, to be big and free, have the house of our dreams and play out our fantasies in real time with big people toys. And back in the day, there were so many movies and role models glamorizing the telling of love and toy story from every point of view.

So we finished our homework and graduated from school, but OMG, homework was easy compared to big people's lot of struggle and strife to pay the bills for that real life fantasy. If only we had known. Maybe we would have enjoyed our youthful play even more and for longer. Now we have to go to work, cook, clean, do dishes, wash clothes and do more homework with that real baby who is now old enough for school. On no, not THAT again.

It's important to remember that a character can only play a "part" of the "whole" in life's divine play of the *Greatest Story Ever Told.*

So, why were we placed on this stage of many parts in a play with countless scenes and props of maya, (illusion)? Why would a loving Creator put us here to labor and even suffer through our roles of seeming independence?

I used to think that maybe the Creator just loves a good story and hopes He/r offspring will eventually reach a happy ending, but maybe that's just a human perception. It is uncanny how we, the offspring, do seem to anticipate a happy ending in every story, especially when the leading character has to climb the highest mountain, is afraid of heights, the journey is fraught with danger and the entire adventure appears impossible.

Now, I'm beginning to think our acts are so questionable because we were blessed with *Free Will* — the right to create our personal view of reality in this 3rd dimension we call "life." Again, *Free Will* allows us the opportunity to choose *Love or Fear.*

The world as we have created is a process of our
thinking. It cannot be changed without
changing our thinking.
— Albert Einstein

So is freedom just another illusion? Maybe, if that's your point of view. If you lose your balance and get stuck in Act 1 believing that's all there is till the end of Act 111, and the beginning of . . .

ACT lV

THE ELDER

"They say" . . . you're too old for dreams.
You don't have enough time left to plant, harvest
and enjoy the fruits of your labor.
If it only takes a 'moment' to spiritually awaken,
what's time got to do with it?

Again, if it's true that "Self realization is our only purpose for BEing" — then it's safe to say Act IV could very well be the justification of our active role on Earth's big, round stage. Of course, there are a number of entrances to Act IV. Maybe you feel you had your chance and blew it, and maybe you did, if you're attached to the average concept of collections and accomplishments as symbols of success. Now you have wrinkles; you're out of shape; you're tired and it just doesn't matter anymore; but again, you are still here and you are reading this book because you are NOT finished. Maybe you are just getting started. Wasn't it the Great Way Shower who said in the midst of performing miracles: "These things ye shall do and even more"? To repeat a familiar phrase: "Are we there yet?"

I can remember when I thought "Awakening" was the Grand Finale, now I realize it's just the Prologue. It reminds me of a time when I thought I had reached the top of a mountain only to discover an even higher range loomed before me, and so . . . I kept climbing.

As for 3D accomplishments — at age 62 Agatha Christie penned the hit play, *Mousetrap*. Now there is some symbolism for you, MOUSETRAP. Following a sell-out run in 2012, **Mousetrap** opened in the West End of London in 1952, and has been running continuously hitting an all time record. Please consider that Michelangelo completed his sculpture, Rodandini Pieta, at 88 years of age. There are many more who defied what "they say," like architect, Frank Lloyd Wright; musician, Arthur Rubinstein; African leader, Nelson Mandela; actor, George Burns; actresses, Betty White and Sophia Loren; fitness expert, Jack LaLanne; superstars, Mick Jagger, Paul McCartney, Ringo Starr and many, many others. Most all of us have heard of them, and most all of them worked, and/or still work well into their 70's, 80's and beyond.

We might think to say: "They are different. They were genius. They were chosen" — but we are all chosen. We are the ones who choose. First, we choose what we think, and what we think determines what we eat, drink, say and do. We choose to be little and insignificant. We choose to be BIG and great. The choice is always OURS.

I recall sitting in a casting office in Hollywood, CA., the result of some lady who had discovered me in a beauty shop. Yes, the dream "to be discovered" did come true from time to time. Anyway, she thought I looked the part of Maria in West Side Story and made all the necessary arrangements for me to meet the casting agents. By the time I reached the studio, I discovered that Natalie Wood had signed a contract to play the part of Maria that very morning. Since the casting agents liked me, they sent me on to a "Cattle Call" type of interview for some commercial. They advised me to lie about my age. I was soon to discover why.

A room full of beautiful young women lined the walls with their slick portfolios full of every type of professional shot required. An artist's rep hurried in to meet with a casting agent. They stood center room directly before me. The casting agent examined the rep's composite. Handing the composite back to him, I overheard him say: "She's a beautiful young woman, John, but she's a has been. How old is she —24 or something?"

OMG! 'I' was 24. Was I already a Has Been? I hadn't even been anything yet. Already I was finished, a predictable has been. It seems once you are beyond your teen years . . . well, you're on your way OUT, at least in Hollywood, proving once again that age is totally relative.

Fulfilling dreams has always been somewhat of an easy phenomenon for me, the best part being that every door I ever knocked on opened to invite me in. After all, that is what I expected, which only proves the concept: "Thinking makes it so." This willed convenience invariably enabled me to peak my curious longing to determine the rewards of each momentary desire.

Unfortunately, or fortunately, the benefits of being on the inside never held my attention for any length of time. The rewards were never quite enough: not enough money, not enough applause, not enough recognition, not enough of anything I thought I needed at the time. Turns out, I was just passing through.

Maybe the Source of BEing was trying to tell me something. Maybe the experience of knocking on all those doors was the only way I could really find what I was looking for — the truth. Maybe it was the only way Spirit could convince a stubborn child like me: "You're not a human form from a temporal realm with an eternal spirit, you're an eternal spirt who borrowed a human form to learn the art of balance in a temporal realm."

You can never feed your soul with mere distractions: glitter, glamour and pretense of the material world will never be enough.

In addition to Michael Jackson, a number of superstars prove that point: Elvis Presley, Marilyn Monroe, and Whitney Houston to name a few. These were trend setting celebrities who had reached the very top of the mountain in a sensational climb. Adored and chased by throngs of worldwide fans, they appeared to have everything; still, they died unfulfilled, drugged and alone. More recently, one of America's most revered funny men, Robin Williams, desperate and distraught, hung himself to die alone.

On September, 4, 2014, America's beloved funny girl, Joan Rivers, died as a result of a sudden cardiac arrest during a simple medical procedure in a doctor's office. Joan used to say that what she considered death was an empty calendar. That would mean no one needed her, so she filled that calendar with one engagement after another, proving the power house she was till the very end at 81.

So, if you are lucky enough to get to Act IV, surely you will realize you have just entered another scene on the stage of this great play called *Life*. And that's exactly what Act IV is — another scene and change of costumes with a new part and lines to learn. This book begins with the famous words of the renowned writer, William Shakespeare, who said: "Play your part well."

Problem is, we still don't have any desirable role models in Act IV. The late Mother Teresa, the Dali Lama and the Pope appear to be the only exemplary icons leading to our mission BEfore BEginning. But who can be a Mother Teresa, a Pope or the Dali Lama? How can you package those images in today's commercial scenario of suck-cess?

Again, the media stays focussed on youth, career and the art of "getting" people, places, things. And rightly so, since we eventually grow out of our need to pretend. Just how long are we supposed to be attracted to the pseudo world, to play Santa Claus, the Easter Bunny, and laugh at jokes that aren't funny?

OMG! All those ads, commercials, painted signs, self help books and internet leaders telling us what we want and need in order to *get* "in." Oh, what to do when it's time to turn away from the outside world of distractions? You've been there. No regrets, you did your best with the toys and now you know that's all they were, and are — toys. Maybe that's all you came to realize this time out. So . . . now what?

The Finish Line

Then somehow
It's time to surrender
Our worldly condition
Time to remember our mission
To awaken from the
Dream
To return from
Whence we came, to
LOOK
Through the eyes
Of our heart and
BE
At home in
BLISS
Again

Maybe you graduated from all the hoopla, and now you see how life on Earth is really a refining process, like taking a rough, dull stone through a process of severe cutting, chipping and polishing in order to reveal the sparkling beauty of a diamond within. Maybe we really are, as *they say* — "diamonds in the rough." Maybe we are here to tap into the darkest nature of our deepest fears, that we may learn what's real and the importance of returning to the light of home, BEfore BEginning. Maybe it is time to reach for the sun and *grow UP.*

Meditation & Spiritual Awakening . . .

There are many forms of meditation that can help us tune into the moment and awaken to our natural inheritance of conscious awareness. Deep meditation is a golden key to the daily upkeep of mind, body, youth and eternal life. In spite of what "they say," there are as many paths to spiritual awakening as there are human BEings. There is not one true mantra to follow, just like there is not one true religion, practice, exercise or diet.

Most fail to realize all beliefs are but vehicles to drive along a contemplative journey seeking awareness. Reaching the destination of Pure Consciousness is the real purpose of meditation as opposed to the popular trend of sitting in silence following the breath or a mantra as a means to empty the mind for purposes of relaxation, possible healing and personal gain. It's important to realize that meditation is meant to be a part of life, not a selected time to escape from life.

EPILOGUE

So now you're beyond the age of retirement and maybe even older, finished, according to what "they say." And if you choose to believe life no longer needs you, it doesn't, and won't. You were a seed, a bud, a blossom and now, "they say," you are about to FALL from the tree.

Regardless, your life's journey in this third dimension is all about the choices you made and make. Maybe you see that *Self Realization* IS your true purpose for BEing, or, maybe you always wanted to travel the world stage: go on a faraway trip, buy a new costume, color your hair, try a new face cream and a new lipstick. If you're a guy, you're apt to try a little Viagra, touch up those grays, go to the gym, buy a sports car and flaunt whatever you were able to accomplish during your climb.

You ate of the *Tree of Life* and so you KNOW; and perhaps by now, you know that it's not enough to know, so you continue to hear that little voice inside that cries loud and clear: "You're not finished yet. You have yet to complete your earthly sojourn. Don't buy into that Old Age stuff. Be like a cloud; rise above it. You always knew you would live forever, and that's because you will."

Maybe after all this time you have finally realized that to return to your origin is a process of purification, a process guiding you to BE even more than you ever imagined. You intuitively knew this as a small child running wild with enthusiastic joy.

You knew to accept your youthful awareness as a part of your package.

Remember when they used to talk about aging gracefully? They don't talk about that anymore, only about the latest remedies to hide your years for continued acceptance in the Material World. Speaking of the Material World — I recall being a twelve year old coveting a stack of home magazines tucked safely away on a shelf in my parents' closet. The magazines were special — a collection I had been savoring for a long time.

Turning each page slowly, my eyes would devour each picture setting. My mind would dream of having my own space to decorate, and my heart would long. I never really had a room of my own, except for the dinette with my bed in it, and before that, another dinette with all my toys in it. Neither room had a door. I was too young to think about becoming a designer/decorator. I didn't even realize they existed; yet, when I grew up, I taught myself to be one.

Just recently, I closed my bank account for *Gabrielle, EastWest Interiors* — a major *letting go* of an image and career I had nurtured for most of my adult life. Both residential and commercial venues have been explored in vast experience. I'm NOT RETIRED, as I explained to the nice lady at the Driver's License Administration, I'm simply moving on to another means of self expression. Now that I've knocked on enough doors, and know what's inside, *Self Realization* is the final door. For more insight into my personal experiences, please read my book, "Destiny's Moment of Forever" — an eBook available on Amazon.

My husband, Rob, and I departed for Egypt on Oct. 29, 2014. We indulged on a pilgrimage to the ancient past. We toured all the powerful pyramids and temples with spiritual guides and a private Egyptologist. The Journey offered ascension and the promise of opening doors to awareness via pyramid power. In one way I feel lame — like I'm still searching outside myself, but then, that's just a role I'm playing in this, my personal journey of seeking my impersonal self . . . *BEfore BEginning.*

*"Seek the wisdom of
the ages, but look at the world
through the eyes of a child."*
— *Anonymous*

The Cleansing

Beloved . . .
open your mind
to the waters of Source

Allow your BEing
the gift of Divine Love

Allow
yourself to bathe in
gratitude and forgiveness
and in that Spirit
do whatever you are called to do
right then, and right there in that
moment with no thought
of loss or gain

Know you are touched by the
ONE
to receive greater gifts
than you ever imagined
here, now, in the
PRESENT

Know also
that as you have
been GIVEN you
are free to
GIVE
them all away

MORE

Gabrielle remembers when she thought aging was something that would never happen to her. She would say: "By the time I reach 50, that 'Forever Young' pill will have been discovered and available." Now, in 2016, in spite of all advancements, most all agree that aging is an inevitable culprit everyone is destined to endure. Whatever your aliment, it's something to be expected, especially if you are over 40. But what if aging is an old paradigm? Science is the first to admit that most all discoveries are in a state of flux, that each new discovery becomes lost in the latest find. Here, I'm reminded of my lifelong quest of *searching for truths that don't lie.*

When Gabrielle mentioned this concept to a medical doctor, he was shocked. "You mean you don't believe you will ever die?" He smirked, shaking his head in disbelief. "Of course you will die, eventually, but what if it's not from old age? What if old age is just a concept we've all agreed upon? What if this predictable phenomenon is controllable? What if old age is just an accumulation of toxic waste collected from years of bad decisions — the result of eating bad food, drinking contaminated water, breathing polluted air and thinking based on fear due to lack of awareness? What if you could grow a limb like geckos grow their tails back? Bottom line, what if you just changed your mind?"

ADDITIONAL INSPIRATION

Below, please find a number of books I have found to be extremely inspiring towards maintaining a healthy attitude and approach to spiritual, mental and physical well being beginning with my own experience story:

Gabrielle Olivier
"DESTINY'S MOMENT OF FOREVER"
available on Amazon.

James Allen, AS A MAN THINKETH

Joseph S. Benner, THE IMPERSONAL LIFE

Echart Tolle, THE POWER OF NOW

Maureen Edwardson, YOUR MAGICAL EVOLUTIONARY CODE UNLEASHED

Greg Braden, THE SPONTANEOUS HEALING OF BELIEF

Masuro Emoto, HIDDEN MESSAGES IN WATER

Dr. Paul Pearsall, THE PLEASURE PRESCRIPTION

Dr. Jan McBarron, CURCUMIN, The 21st Century Cure

Dr Joe Dispenza, YOU ARE THE PLACEBO

Maintaining youth

is not a means

of acquiring anything

of wearing a beautiful mask

of dancing at the ball or marching

in the parade.

Maintaining youth

is a state of awareness.

— Gabrielle

Rob and I went to the
Driver's License
Administration today.

We asked for the lady
who inspired this book.

We were told
she no longer worked there.
She had *retired.*

*Printed & Published by BookBaby
in the USA*